THE DOLLAR ENDGAME

Hyperinflation Is Coming

Peruvian Bull

CONTENTS

Introduction

I am getting increasingly worried about the number of warning signals that are flashing red for hyperinflation. I believe the process has already begun, as I will lay out in this paper. The first stages of hyperinflation begin slowly, and as this is an exponential process, most people will not grasp the true extent of it until it is too late.

The United States is at the end of a massive debt super cycle. This 80 to 100 year pattern always ends in one of two scenarios; default/restructuring (deflation such as the Great Depression), or inflation (in severe cases, hyperinflation such as the Weimar Republic). The United States has been abusing its privilege as the world reserve currency holder to enforce its political and economic hegemony onto the third world, specifically by creating massive artificial demand for Treasuries and U.S. dollars. This has allowed the United States to borrow extraordinary amounts of money at extremely low rates for decades, creating a Sword of Damocles that hangs over the global financial system. The massive debt loads have been transferred worldwide, and sovereigns are starting to call our bluff. Systemic risk within the domestic financial system has built up to the point that collapse is all but inevitable, and the Federal Reserve has demonstrated it will do whatever it takes to defend legacy finance including banks, broker/dealers, and government solvency, even at the expense of the US dollar.

A NEW ROME

The Global Monetary System

"In their masterwork tapestry entitled "Allegory of the Prisoner's Dilemma" the artists Diaz Hope and Roth visually depict a great tower of civilization that rests upon a bedrock of human cooperation and competition across history. The artists force us to confront the fact that after 10,000 years of human civilization we are now at a cross-roads. Today we have the highest living standards in human history that co-exists with an ability to destroy our planet ecologically and ourselves through nuclear war.

We are in the greatest period of stability with the largest probabilistic tail risk ever. The majority of Americans have lived their entire lives without ever experiencing a direct war and this is, by all accounts, rare in the history of humankind. Does this mean we are safe? Or does the risk exist in some other form, transmuted and changed by time and space, unseen by most political pundits who brazenly tout perpetual American dominance across our screens?"[1]

The Bretton Woods Agreement

Money functions as a unit of account, a medium of exchange, and a store of wealth (typically called the three-factor definition of money). Historically, money was one of the first technologies produced in agrarian societies as a means of transferring value from one party to another, across space and time. Many things have been money: shells, beads, coins made of gold and silver, oil, pebbles, and more. Money enables the advancement of economic growth through the elimination of the double coincidence of wants, and provides the ability to storehouse value over long periods of time. Since the inception of world trade, merchants have attempted to use a single form of money for international settlement. From the 1500s-1700s, the Spanish silver peso (where we derive the $ sign) was the standard; by the 1800s and early 1900s, the British rose to prominence and the pound (under a gold standard) became the de facto world reserve currency, helping to project the United Kingdom's military and economic dominance over much of the world. After World War 1, geopolitical power started to shift to the United States, and this was cemented in 1944 at Bretton Woods, where the U.S. was designated as the world reserve currency holder.

In the early fall of 1939, the world had watched in horror as the German blitzkrieg raced through Poland, conquering the entire territory in 35 days. This was no easy task, as the Polish army numbered more than 1,500,000 men, and was thought by military tacticians to be a tough adversary, even for the industrious German war machine. As WWII continued to heat up and country after country fell to the German onslaught, European countries, fretting over possible invasions of their countries and annexation of their gold, started sending massive amounts of their gold reserves to the US. At one point, the Federal Reserve held over 50% of all above-ground reserves in the world.[2]

U.S. Gold Reserves and U.S. Goods Trade Balance: 1878-2018

SOURCES: National Bureau of Economic Research, World Bank, measuringworth.com, U.S. Bureau of Economic Analysis, World Trade Historical Database and authors' calculations.

■ FEDERAL RESERVE BANK OF ST. LOUIS

In a global monetary system restrained by a gold standard, countries must hold gold reserves in their vaults in order to issue paper currency. The European nations all exited the gold standard via executive acts during the dark days of the Great Depression (in Germany's case, immediately after World War I) and during the buildup to World War II by their respective finance ministers. However, the understanding was they would return to the gold standard, or at least some form of it, after the chaos had subsided. As the conflict wound down, and it became clear that the Allies would win, the Western powers understood that they would need to come to a new consensus on the creation of a novel global monetary and economic system.

Britain, the previous world superpower, was marred by the war, and had seen most of her industrial cities ruined by the blitz. France was basically in tatters, with most infrastructure completely obliterated by German shelling during various points of the war. The leaders of the Western world looked ahead to a long road of rebuilding and recovery. The new threat of the U.S.S.R. loomed heavy on the horizon, as the Iron Curtain was already taking shape within the territories re-conquered by the hordes of the Red Army. Realizing that it was unsafe to send the gold back from the U.S., they understood that a post-war economic system would need a new world reserve currency. The U.S. was the de-facto choice as it had massive gold reserves and huge lending capacity due to its untouched infrastructure and incredibly productive economy.

At Bretton Woods, a consortium of nations assented to an agreement whereby the dollar would become the world reserve currency and the participating nations would synchronize monetary policy to avoid competitive devaluation. In summary, they could still redeem dollars for gold at a fixed rate of $35 an oz, a hard redemption peg which the U.S. would defend.[3] Thus they entered into a quasi- gold standard, where citizens and private corporations could not redeem dollars for gold (due to the Gold Reserve Act, c. 1934), but sovereign governments via the central banks could. Since their currencies (like the franc and pound) were pegged to the dollar, and the dollar pegged to gold, all countries remained connected indirectly to a gold standard, stabilizing their currency conversion rate to each other and limiting local governments' ability to print and spend recklessly.

For a few decades, this system worked well enough. American economic growth spurred European rebuilding, and world trade continued to boom. Cracks started to appear during the Guns and Butter era of the 1960's, when Vietnam War spending and Johnson's great society programs spurred a new era of fiscal profligacy. The United States started borrowing massively, and dollars in the form of Treasuries started stacking up in foreign central banks' reserve accounts.

French president Charles De Gaulle did the calculus and realized in 1965 that the U.S. had issued far too many dollars, even considering the massive gold reserves they had, to ever redeem all dollars for gold. He laid out this argument in his infamous Criterion Speech and began aggressively redeeming dollars for gold. The global "run on the dollar" had already begun, but the process accelerated after his seminal address, as every large sovereign turned in their fiat for bullion, and the U.S. Treasury was forced to start massively exporting gold. Backing the sovereign governments' actions were fiscal and monetary strategists getting more and more worried that the U.S. would not have enough gold to redeem their dollars, and they would be left holding a bag of worthless paper dollars, backed by nothing but promises. The outward trickle of gold quickly became a deluge, and policymakers at all levels of Treasury and State Department started to worry.

Nearing a dollar solvency crisis, Richard Nixon announced on August 15th, 1971, that he was closing the gold window, effectively barring all countries from current and future gold redemptions.[4] Money ceased to be based on the gold in the Treasury vaults, and instead was now completely unbacked, based solely on government decree, or fiat. Fixed wage and price controls were created, inflation skyrocketed, and unemployment spiked. Nixon's speech was not as well received internationally as it was in the United States. Many in the global community saw Nixon's plan as a unilateral action and an implicit default on American obligations. In response, the Group of Ten (G-10) industrialized democracies decided on new exchange rates based on a devalued dollar in an agreement known as the Smithsonian Agreement. This plan went into effect in December 1971, but it was unsuccessful. Starting in February 1973, speculative market pressure caused the US dollar to devalue, leading to a series of exchange parities.

Amid still-heavy pressure on the dollar in March of that year, the G–10 implemented a strategy that called for six European members to tie their currencies together and jointly float them against the dollar. That decision essentially brought an end to the fixed exchange rate system established by Bretton Woods. This crisis came to be known as the "Nixon Shock" and the DXY (U.S. dollar index) began to fall in global markets. See the chart below for reference.[5]

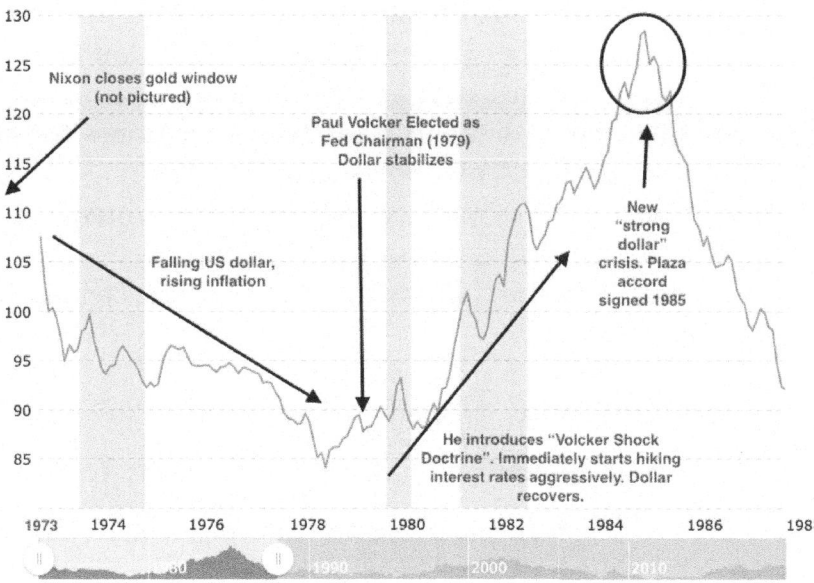

This crisis came out of the blue for most members of the administration. Inflation began ripping higher while the economy contracted, a phenomenon known as stagflation. According to Keynesian economists, stagflation was literally impossible, as it was a violation of the Phillips Curve principle, where unemployment and inflation were inversely correlated. Thus inflation should theoretically be decreasing as the recession worsened and unemployment climbed through 1973-1975.

Phillips Curve Explained:
- Low Unemployment means lots of jobs/high demand for labor.
- Thus, more workers are employed, and wages rise- putting more money in more people's pockets.

- These people go out and purchase market products due to their higher propensity to spend, (what economist John Maynard Keynes called aggregate demand) and this higher demand leads to higher prices for goods and services. This shows up as inflation.
- Consider the opposite- high unemployment leads to fewer jobs and less money for people.
- Less demand for goods and services creates lower inflation.

Keynesian economists treated this curve as a law of nature, rather than a general rule. We see exceptions to this rule everywhere- Argentina is a prime example, where they have persistently high unemployment and high inflation. These economists were utterly blindsided by the emergence of this phenomena.

After the closing of the gold window in 1971, the crisis spread, inflation kept climbing, and other sovereigns began contemplating devaluing their currencies as their only peg, the U.S. dollar, was now unmoored and looked to be heading to disaster. American exports started climbing (due to a cheaper dollar, foreigners could now import to their countries), straining export economies and sparking talks of a currency war. Knowing they had to do something to stop the bleeding, the Nixon administration, at the direction of Henry Kissinger, made a secret deal with OPEC, creating what is now called the Petrodollar system.

To summarize:

"The 1973 oil crisis further fixed the value of the dollar as a result of this oil shock, bringing Saudi Arabia and the OPEC countries to make a secret agreement with Washington, the main architect being President Nixon's legendary Secretary of State Mr. Henry Kissinger. This agreement provided that in exchange for Washington's political and military protection, the OPEC countries would be required to sell oil only in dollars. The Petrodollar was thus born, being a replacement for the gold-linked standard that existed prior to Nixon. Once this system was supported by OPEC members, the global demand for US petrodollars hit an all-time high. Petrodollars became the basis for American domination over the global financial system which resulted in other countries being forced to buy dollars in order to get oil on the international market."[6]

Petrodollars, or U.S. dollars paid to a country exporting oil in exchange for the commodity, have existed since the late 1940s, but were only used by a few suppliers. This new action by Kissinger coerced the largest oil producers to adopt this system. The petrodollar system is essentially an exchange of oil for U.S. dollars between countries that import oil and those that produce it. By requiring most of the oil producers in the world to price contracts in dollars, the petrodollar system created artificial demand for dollars, which helped to support the value of the U.S. dollar on foreign exchange markets. This system generates surpluses for oil producers, leading to large reserves of U.S. dollars for oil exporters, which need to be reinvested in some way, such as through loans or direct investment in the United States. Thus, it implicitly backs dollars with oil.

But it still wasn't enough. Inflation, like many things, had inertia, and the oil shocks caused by the Yom Kippur War and other geo-political events continued to strain the economy through the 1970's. Please review the graph below per the St Louis Fed for reference:[7]

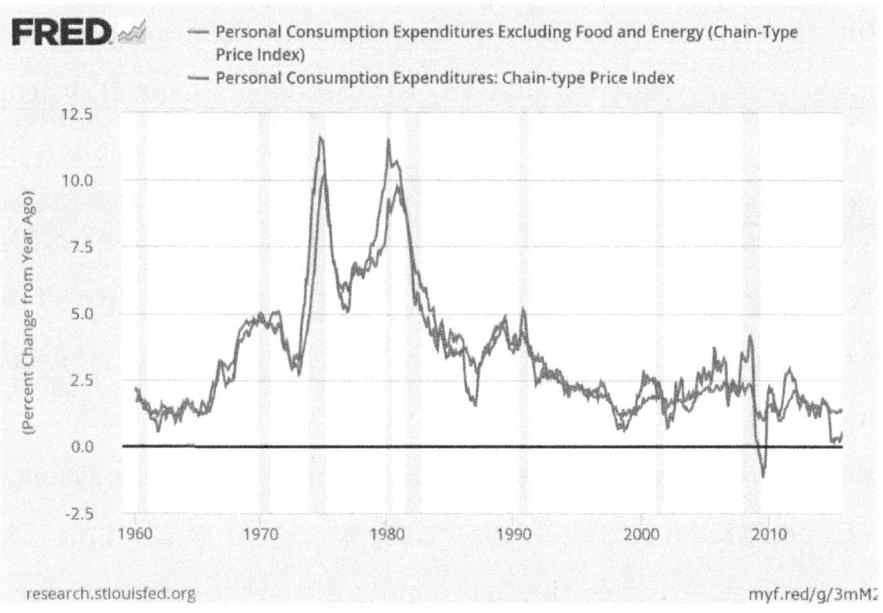

Running out of road, monetary policymakers finally decided to employ the nuclear option. Paul Volcker, the new Federal Reserve Chairman selected in 1979, knew that it was imperative to break the back of inflation to preserve the global economic system. That year, inflation was spiking well above 10% and continued to climb, with no end in sight. He decided to take drastic action and induced what was later called the "Volcker Shock". To fight the rising inflation, he raised the Fed Funds rate to 20% by March 1980. Inflation remained high, and thus he held the rate at 20% in December and higher than 16% until May of the next year. This severe tightening was in the end able to break the back of inflation, but it also induced a recession.

By hiking interest rates aggressively, consumer credit lending slowed, mortgages became more expensive to finance, and corporate debt became more expensive to borrow. Foreign companies that had been dumping dollar holdings as inflation had risen now had good reason to keep their funds vested in U.S. accounts. When the Petrodollar system, which had started taking shape in '73 was completed in March 1979 under the U.S.-Saudi Joint Commission, the dollar finally began to stabilize.[8]

The worst of the crisis was over.

Volcker had to keep interest rates elevated well above 8% for most of the decade, to shore up support for the dollar and assure foreign creditors that the Fed would do whatever it takes to defend the value of the dollar in the future. These absurdly high interest rates put a brake to U.S. government borrowing, at least for a few years. Foreign creditors breathed a sigh of relief as they saw that the Fed would go to extreme lengths to preserve the value of the dollar and ensure that Treasury bonds paid back their principal + interest in real terms.

Over the next 40 years, the United States and most of the developed world saw a prolonged period of economic growth and global trade. Fiat money became the norm, and creditors accepted the new paradigm, with its new risk of inflation/ devaluation. The global monetary system now consisted of free-floating fiat currencies, liberated from the fetters of the gold reserve system.

Dollar Hegemony

Let us say you are the president of a country like Liberia, a small West African nation, looking to enter global trade. You go talk to the International Monetary Fund, whose economists tell you in order to be a modern economy you need to have your own currency. Thus, you need a central bank to print your own currency (LD), which will be used as legal tender, enforced by your government. Your central bank will act as a lender of last resort for all the commercial and investment banks in your country and will be responsible for stabilizing monetary policy.

But there's an issue - the economists tell you that you cannot have your central bank store up your own currency as the majority of its foreign exchange reserves. They explain that if your currency comes under attack in the global forex markets, you will have to defend it. When the currency trade value is too high, it's easy to fight- you just print your own currency and buy Euros (EU) or Dollars (USD), flooding the market with your currency and taking other currencies out of the market- "devaluing your currency". However, if the inverse is true, and your currency is losing value in the market, printing more to flood the market will only make it worse. You need a stable currency, like bullets in the chamber, to utilize to buy your currency at the market rate, to support its value and drive it back up. A so-called "reserve" currency. This form of currency defense is called "defending the peg" (post-1971, the peg is floating, so it's more of a range, but it's still referred to loosely as a peg).

This exact phenomenon played out during the Asian Financial Crisis of 1997, a classic case study in global monetary crises. Thailand had grown rapidly as world trade boomed in the 1980s and 90s, and its corporate and real estate sectors took on massive amounts of debt. A massive real estate and financial bubble formed. Soon, the bubble started to pop.

The Thai central bank was forced to act and devalue the Thai baht against the US dollar. This decision came after months of downward pressure on the baht due to speculation, which had significantly reduced Thailand's official foreign exchange reserves. This event marked the start of a severe financial crisis in much of East Asia. In the following months, Thailand's currency, stock, and property markets weakened further as the country's problems developed into a dual balance-of-payments and banking crisis. Malaysia, the Philippines, and Indonesia also allowed their currencies to weaken significantly in response to market pressures, with Indonesia eventually experiencing a financial and political crisis.

As the president of Liberia, you see what can happen when a country, especially a small third-world country, doesn't have enough dollar reserves to defend its own currency. Rippling currency devaluations, inflation, social and political unrest, widening economic inequality- the beginning of a death spiral of a country if you aren't careful. So, you tell the IMF that you agree to their terms. They impress upon you that you need to get your bank to buy up some other stable currency to hold as reserves, to defend against this very scenario. As the U.S. dollar is the world reserve currency, you're going to hold it as the majority of your reserve position.

We've established the need for a small country to hold another currency on their balance sheet. If one small country does this, there is little impact on the U.S. dollar. However, under the current system, virtually every country has a central bank, and they all use the dollar as their main reserve currency.[9] This creates massive buying pressure on Treasuries. Using Liberia as an example, the process works like this:

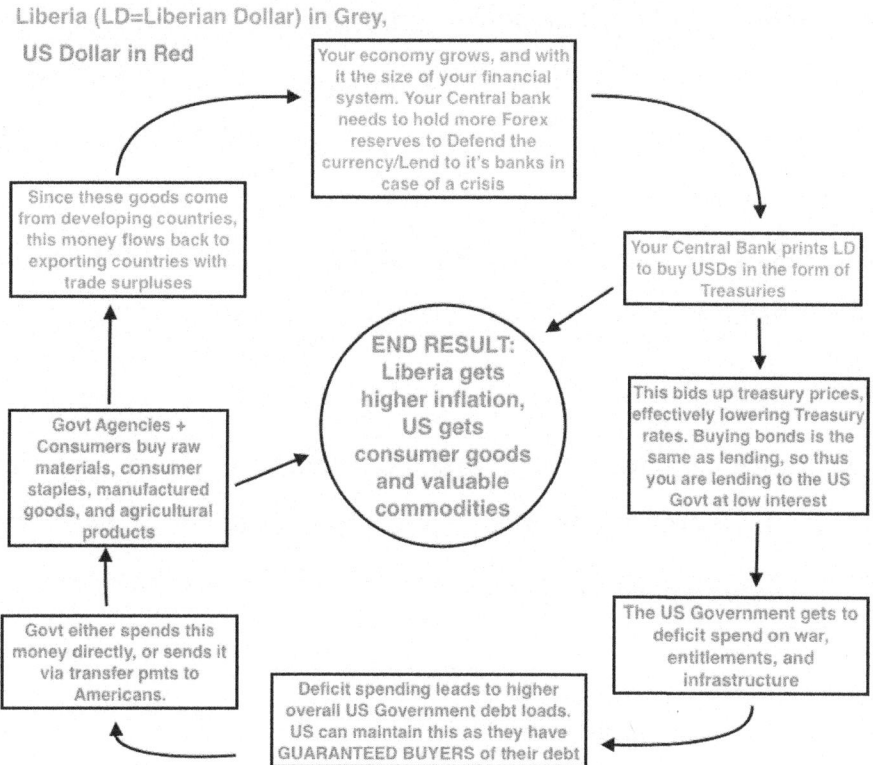

Liberia (LD=Liberian Dollar) in Grey,
US Dollar in Red

Your economy grows, and with it the size of your financial system. Your Central bank needs to hold more Forex reserves to Defend the currency/Lend to it's banks in case of a crisis

Since these goods come from developing countries, this money flows back to exporting countries with trade surpluses

Your Central Bank prints LD to buy USDs in the form of Treasuries

END RESULT: Liberia gets higher inflation, US gets consumer goods and valuable commodities

Govt Agencies + Consumers buy raw materials, consumer staples, manufactured goods, and agricultural products

This bids up treasury prices, effectively lowering Treasury rates. Buying bonds is the same as lending, so thus you are lending to the US Govt at low interest

Govt either spends this money directly, or sends it via transfer pmts to Americans.

The US Government gets to deficit spend on war, entitlements, and infrastructure

Deficit spending leads to higher overall US Government debt loads. US can maintain this as they have GUARANTEED BUYERS of their debt

This is what French Finance Minister Valéry Giscard d'Estaing meant when during the 1960's he had contemptuously called this benefit the US enjoyed "le privilège exorbitant", or the "Exorbitant privilege".[10] He understood that the United States would never face a balance of payments crisis (*AS LONG AS THE USD IS THE WORLD RESERVE CURRENCY*) due to forced buying of Treasuries (from foreign central and commercial banks) and dollars (from Petrodollar system). The US could borrow cheaply, spend lavishly, and not pay for it immediately. <u>Instead, the payment for this privilege would build up in the form of debt and dollars overseas, held by foreigners all around the world.</u> One day, the piper must be paid- but as long as the music is playing, and the punchbowl is out, everyone gets to party, dance & drink to their hearts' content, and the US can remain the belle of the ball.

Effectively, the US can print money, and get real goods. This means we can import consumer products for cheap, and the inflation we create gets exported to other countries. (This is one of the reasons why developing countries tend to have higher inflation).

Another way to explain it:[11]

1. "The US Federal Reserve lowers interest rates or creates

dollars through quantitative easing-both of which are aimed at increasing the total supply of dollars in the world.

2. The Fed's actions allow cheaper dollar credit to be accessed by the US Federal Government, US companies, and those with connections to American banks. When this credit is used by taking out loans, new dollars are created.

3. Those who receive new dollars spend them- often on imports to the US- and the extra dollars end up circulating in foreign countries.

4. Now, foreign countries are flooded with new dollars and their governments face a choice:

5. Let their own currency appreciate in value against the dollar, which would reduce the country's competitiveness in the world market and decrease their exports.

6. Create more of their own currency to stabilize its value against the dollar and retain competitiveness on the world market. However, this causes price inflation for their citizens and makes imports more expensive."

As it is the reserve currency, other countries' central banks need to have U.S. dollars on their balance sheet. Thus, the United States must run persistent current account deficits in order to send out more dollars to the global system, on net, than it receives back. A major byproduct is constant large and increasing trade deficits for the world reserve currency holder (in a fiat money system).

For reference, a current account is the total sum of flows of money into a country. If more money is flowing in, they have a positive current account, and if more is flowing out, then it is negative. Trade deficits are a typical symptom of a current account deficit. See the graph below for an illustration of the U.S. trade deficit over time.[12]

Figure 1

The U.S. Trade Deficit

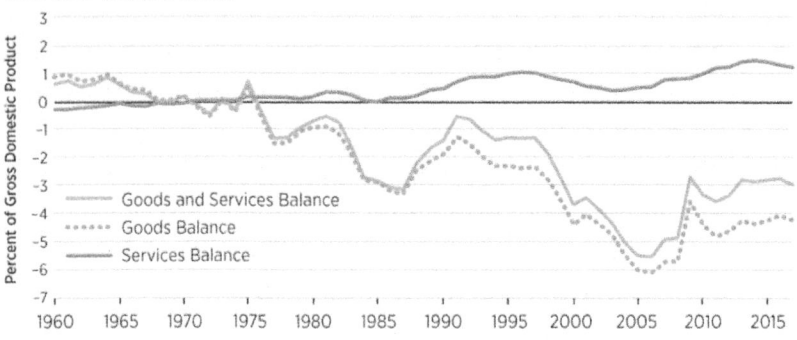

NOTE: Though having a long-running trade deficit in goods, the U.S. has posted a growing surplus in services, such as in travel and finance. This has tempered the size of the overall trade deficit.

SOURCES: Bureau of Economic Analysis, Haver Analytics and authors' calculations.

■ FEDERAL RESERVE BANK OF ST. LOUIS

This is what is known as Triffin's dilemma: the world reserve currency must run constant trade deficits. There are no immediate negative impacts, but in the long run this process is unsustainable, as the host country becomes unproductive (ever wonder why American manufacturing left) because the system forces the reserve currency owner to be a net importer. As world trade grows, the current account deficit/trade deficit grows, and the benefits (more goods to the U.S.) and drawbacks (more dollars build up overseas) increase over time. Eventually the imbalance becomes so great that something snaps, just like it did for the pound post WWI, where policymakers chose the route of deflation in 1921, creating a great depression for the United Kingdom long before America ever experienced it.

Therefore I found it ironic when I heard Trump rail against our trade deficits in one of the 2016 presidential debates. He clearly did not understand how our system works, and that this issue was beneficial in the short term, but detrimental in the long term. Our trade deficits were symptoms of our system working exactly as intended. In fact, a large part of the reason why he was elected was the de-industrialization of the American heartland, where loss of economic vitality from manufacturing jobs was leading to rampant drug abuse, depression, and societal decay. I knew this process of de-industrialization would only get worse with time, and nothing he did (short of taking us off the reserve status) would change that.

Fast forward to today- after decades of this process playing out, foreign central banks collectively hold huge amounts of forex reserves - 62% of which are in U.S. dollars![13]

The majority of the dollar reserves exist mainly in the form of Treasuries, T-bills, and other U.S. government debt. Furthermore, the dollar continues to dominate global trade through the SWIFT network (Society for Worldwide Interbank Financial Telecommunication). SWIFT is a payments system used by multinational banks, institutions, and corporations to settle trade worldwide. USD is the preferred payment method within the system, thus forcing other countries to adopt the dollar in international trade. This is one of the results of the petrodollar system I described earlier. Petrodollars originally were exclusively used to refer to oil contracts priced in USD from Saudi Arabia, but over time the name grew to mean any oil contract, transacted by non-US countries, using the US dollar as the denomination.

When Chile and South Africa trade copper, for example, they have to transact in dollars, because a SWIFT member bank in South Africa will not accept Chilean Pesos as payment, as there is a smaller, less liquid market for it and it doesn't want to take a trading loss when converting to a more usable currency. The contract itself is priced in USD, so if that merchant bank wants to sell it, they can quickly find a buyer. In fact, SWIFT itself published a report in 2014, and found that the USD accounts for almost 80% of all world trade![14]

This process is called dollarization, whereby the dollar is used as the medium of exchange for a contract, in place of some other currency, even between non-U.S. trading partners (Germany and China for example). Dollarization (capital D) of a country occurs when a government switches from managing their own currency to just using the U.S. dollar for trade settlement and tax revenue- like Ecuador, El Salvador, and Panama have done. The U.S. dollar reserves from the petro-dollar system show up on the balance sheets of these overseas financial institutions; they are called Eurodollars, and these USD denominated deposits are not under the direct jurisdiction of the Treasury or Federal Reserve. In 2016, the total value of the Eurodollar market was estimated to be around 13.83 trillion.[15]

Through this process, the United States was able to become the largest and most dominant military force in the history of man, able to fight simultaneous two-theater wars with overseas supply lines. The Treasury could borrow and spend, unimpeded by the normal constraints of market discipline that were hoisted on other countries. Despite not declaring war since 1941, the U.S. has been in a state of near-continuous warfare.

America has defended this system at all costs, even going so far as to directly invade and occupy the Middle East in the Gulf War in 1991 and the Iraq/Afghanistan War (2001-2021). As a result, there are over 800 U.S. military bases around the world, in locales ranging from Turkey to Japan. American institutions like the Senate, Presidency, and Courts were modeled after their Roman antecedents, to the point that the American symbol, the Eagle, is the spitting image of the Roman Aquila adorned on the standard of the centurions.

Most scholars tout the story of Rome as a tale of triumphalism; of valiant centurions battling in the steppes of Asia, of brilliant generals laying traps for enemy armies, of scheming senators fighting battles of political intrigue, and of a sophisticated and well-functioning empire that harnessed engineering to create marvels such as the Colosseum and the Aqueducts.

More sober historians, however, point out that the story of Rome is one that also echoes a warning through the annals of history. A complex society, with mighty political, legal, and financial institutions, supported by a massive military, fell not to a crushing enemy invasion, but to collapse and decay from within. An elite ruling class, detached from the realities of daily life of the citizens, oversaw an empire with growing income inequality, political corruption, and economic despair, and did nothing to stop it.

The Roman Treasury, facing insurmountable debts from years of fruitless war, started "clipping coins", an early form of currency debasement that led to the Roman denarii losing 25% of its value every year. This eventually led to uprisings in Roman provinces and the sacking of Rome - the coup de grace, the final nail in the coffin for what had become the decadent Western Roman Empire.

If the United States loses world reserve currency status, two things happen. First, foreign central banks start massively dumping their huge Treasury/Dollar debt positions due to the loss of utility in holding a failing reserve asset. Next, SWIFT member banks who hold USDs for cross-border payments (Eurodollars) decide to liquidate them as the currency uses utility and a new reserve currency emerges.

This is the one of the many Swords of Damocles hanging over the global financial system. The unraveling of these massive currency and bond positions would truly be catastrophic. Interest rates could effectively jump to +30% or more overnight, creating an immediate solvency crisis for the U.S. government and most banks, corporations, and state governments who rely on low interest rate borrowing. DXY would be whipsawed violently upwards for a period before being forced downward by massive selling pressure from the Eurodollar market. Other currencies would be pulled higher and then lower in volatile moves matching the worst days of the early Nixon crisis. But this is only part of the story. We will come back to this later.

America as a world reserve currency holder is allowed to borrow almost indefinitely without immediate consequence, but this creates massive amounts of U.S. dollar debts overseas. The last time global creditors started to lose faith in the dollar, we saw massive inflation, unemployment, and stagnation domestically, in a period of rapid demographic and economic growth in the rest of the world. If creditors become worried again, and signs are showing up that they are, the results could be catastrophic.

THE OUROBOROS

Derivatives and the Alchemy of Risk

"The Ouroboros, a Greek word meaning "tail devourer", is the ancient symbol of a snake consuming its own body in perfect symmetry. The imagery of the Ouroboros evokes the concept of the infinite nature of creation from destruction. The sign appears across cultures and is an important icon in the esoteric tradition of Alchemy. Egyptian mystics first derived the symbol from a real phenomenon in nature.

In extreme heat a snake, unable to self-regulate its body temperature, will experience an out-of-control spike in its metabolism. In a state of mania, the snake is unable to differentiate its own tail from its prey, and will attack itself, self-cannibalizing until it perishes. In nature and markets, when randomness self-organizes itself into too perfect symmetry, order becomes the source of chaos, and chaos feeds on itself."[16]

Random Walks and Portfolio Insurance

In financial markets, traders have long looked for mathematical relationships between and within assets, to aid in speculation and price prediction. As data aggregation improved, and information became more widely distributed in the 1930s and 1940s, financial analysts quickly realized that the stock market, as well as individual securities, followed Bell Curve distributions, at least in most time periods. The idea of Brownian motion, which refers to the random movement of particles within a fluid, arose from the concept of random events. In the mid-1800s, scientist Robert Brown observed that the movements of these particles within a fluid were completely unpredictable and appeared to be random. These movements, known as Brownian motion, were characterized by a lack of discernible pattern or order.

Drawing on Brownian motion, mathematicians had created Probability Theory, which could estimate the given probability (not certainty) of a set of outcomes. As an analogy, predicting the result of an individual coin toss accurately every time is essentially impossible, but if you do it 100 times, Probability Theory will tell you that you have a very high probability of 50 heads and 50 tails, or something close to it (45/55 or 53/47 for example). The likelihood of 95 heads and 5 tails, an extreme outlier, would be very close to 0. This is because there is a 50% probability of either heads or tails- and thus the distribution of 100-coin flips should roughly match this probability. This theory of randomness of prices as it applied to finance came to be known as the Random Walk Theory- and predicted that prices were basically completely unpredictable. Understanding this concept, traders in the 1960s observed that the probability was great that returns on a single equity security would hover between some set performance range, like -10% and +10%. Rarely did the return hit the extreme ends of the curve. It didn't matter what the time period was, 1 day, 1 month, or 1 year, the traders always had trouble reliably predicting a single exact future movement (like predicting heads/tails on a single coin toss) but could reliably say what the probability of variance over time (outcome of 100 coin tosses) would be, and map this mathematical distribution on a bell curve.

These Bell Curve distributions, after being modified for applications in financial markets, came to be known as Value At Risk (VaR) models. Over the course of the 1960s and 1970s, these models came to be widely used in the asset management industry.[17] Essentially what these VaR models could do was provide a statistical technique used to measure the amount of potential loss that could happen in an investment portfolio over a specified period. Value at Risk gives the probability of losing more than a given amount in each portfolio.

These models have "skinny tails", that is to say, they predict the likelihood of extreme events (standard deviation of 3 or more, or outside 99.7% of the curve) happening as very low, especially on the downside. Outlier events were thus coined "tail risk", occurrences that only show up on the far tails of the distribution. These models were built using the recorded historical prices of thousands of commodities, equities, and bonds. For earlier markets, they would even plug in estimates created by econometricians (i.e., corn prices in 1430) to arrive at a large enough data set. With this data, asset managers could feel safe utilizing leverage and complex derivatives in risky investments, as these models told them that the likelihood of severe losses (-30% for example) in a single day was near-zero.

At the same time, Eugene Fama, an American economist freshly minted with a PhD from the University of Chicago, developed his Efficient Markets Hypothesis in early 1970. Drawing on the random walk theory, Fama posited that since stock movements were random, it was impossible to "beat the market". Current market prices incorporated all available and future information, and thus buying undervalued stocks, or selling at inflated prices, was not feasible. Making consistent profits was impossible- if you made money, you just got "lucky" as the market randomly moved in your favor after you made the trade. The price, therefore, was always "right".

This further increased investor risk appetite. Armed with these two theories, they started making statistical algorithms that modeled the stock market and loaded themselves up with more risk. Starting in the early 1980s, portfolio insurance started to gain traction within the industry. This "insurance" basically was an automated system that short-sold S&P 500 Index futures in case of a market decline. This concept was invented by Hayne Leland and Mark Rubinstein, who started a business named Leland O'Brien Rubinstein Associates (LOR) in 1980, and was developed into a computer program referred to by the same acronym. They were incredibly successful in marketing their risk management system, and by the mid-1980s, hundreds of millions of dollars of Assets Under Management (AUM) from institutions ranging from investment banks to large mutual funds were protected by this new-fangled product.

LOR was a program that engaged in dynamic hedging, which means it would constantly monitor market conditions and adjust its portfolio risk in real time. This type of hedging is currently used by derivative dealers to hedge gamma or vega exposures. It involves constantly adjusting the hedge as the underlying asset moves, often multiple times per day, hence it is referred to as "dynamic." The creators of LOR promoted it as a program that actively works to safeguard a portfolio, a "set and forget" approach that allows portfolio managers and traders to focus on generating alpha rather than worrying about potential losses.

Black Monday- October 19, 1987

During the first half of 1987, stock markets experienced significant growth. By the end of August, the Dow Jones Industrial Average (DJIA) had increased by 39% over the course of seven months, raising concerns about an asset bubble. In mid-October, a series of negative news reports eroded investor confidence and caused additional market instability. The government announced a larger trade deficit than expected, and the value of the dollar decreased. These events signaled the upcoming record losses that occurred a week later.

On October 14, several markets began to suffer large daily losses. On October 16, the continuous selloffs coincided with an event known as "triple witching," which refers to the occurrence of monthly expirations of options and futures contracts on the same day. By the end of the trading day on October 16, which was a Friday, the DJIA had lost 4.6%. The weekend trading break provided only a temporary respite; on Saturday, October 17, Treasury Secretary James Baker publicly threatened to devalue the US dollar in order to reduce the country's growing trade deficit. Then, the unimaginable occurred.[18]

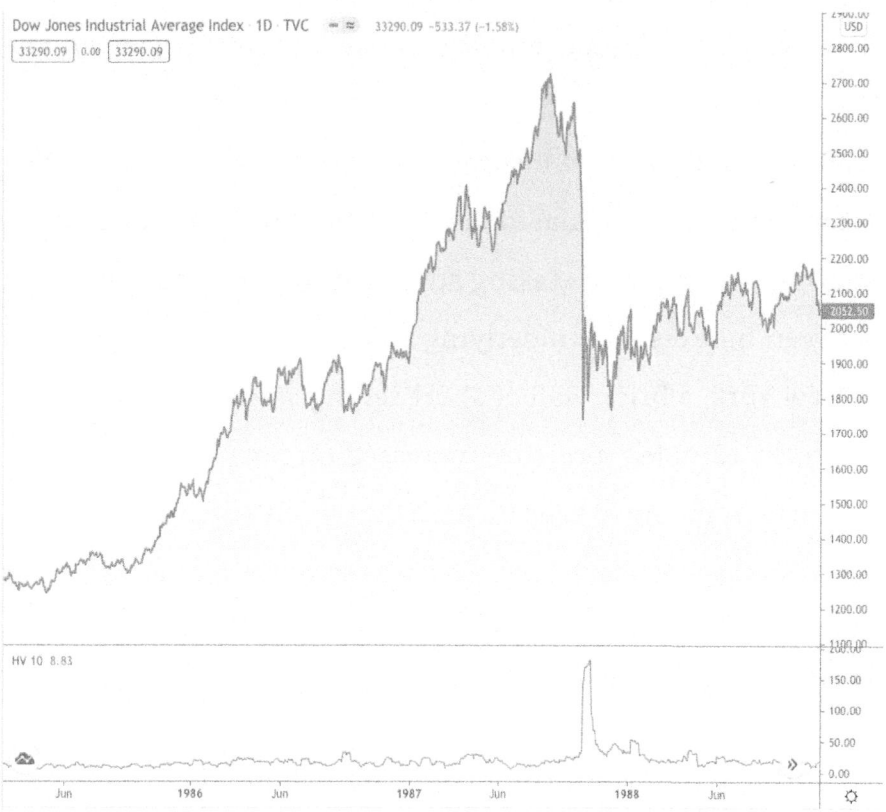

Even before U.S. markets opened for trading on Monday morning, stock markets in Asia began plunging. Additional investors moved to liquidate positions, and the number of sell orders vastly outnumbered willing buyers near previous prices, creating a cascade in stock markets. In the most severe case, New Zealand's stock market fell 60 percent, and would take years to recover. The contagion quickly moved to the United States. Upon market open on the New York Stock Exchange, sell orders came flooding in. Traders reported racing each other to the pits to sell. Author Scott Patterson describes the scene:[19]

"Over the next fifteen minutes before trading began on the NYSE, massive pressure built up on index futures, almost entirely from portfolio insurance firms. The big drop by index futures triggered a signal for another new breed of trader: index arbitrageurs, investors taking advantage of small discrepancies between indexes and underlying stocks. When trading opened in New York, a brick wall of short selling slammed the market. As stocks tumbled, pressure increased on portfolio insurers to sell futures, racing to keep up with the widely gapping market in a devastating feedback loop. The arbs scrambled to put on their trades but were overwhelmed: futures and stocks were falling in unison. Chaos ruled.'"

According to reports from traders on the floor of the New York Stock Exchange, the ticker numbers were moving so quickly that they became unreadable. The market experienced a complete lack of liquidity, with a tsunami of sell orders causing the recording infrastructure to malfunction. The specialists, who were responsible for representing firms and facilitating trades on the floor, stopped answering their phones as they were inundated with calls from institutions seeking to sell. Many stocks were frozen, while others saw a sudden spike in trading volume. Proctor and Gamble, whose stock price was at $6.09 at the end of trading the previous Friday, plummeted to just $0.03. To keep up with the overwhelming demand, market makers resorted to trading based on stock prices from an hour earlier, as the system was overwhelmed by the backlog.

In the United States, this collapse quickly came to be known as "Black Monday", with the DJIA finishing down 508 points, or 22.6 percent. Quoting an article from the Federal Reserve Board:[20]

"There is so much psychological togetherness that seems to have worked both on the up side and on the down side," Andrew Grove, Chief Executive of technology company Intel Corp., said in an interview. "It's a little like a theater where someone yells 'Fire!' (and everybody runs for the exit)". "It felt really scary," said Thomas Thrall, a senior professional at the Federal Reserve Bank of Chicago, who was then a trader at the Chicago Mercantile Exchange. "People started to understand the interconnectedness of markets around the globe. For the first time, investors could watch on live television as a financial crisis spread market to market – in much the same way viruses move through human populations and computer networks."

Black Monday represented a catastrophic rebuttal to the mathematicians and economists who created the Random Walk Theory and Value- At- Risk models. These probability theorists had stated that events like this were improbable- so unlikely in fact that their models predicted Black Monday was basically impossible. Thus, no one in the market had hedged or expected an event as extreme as this. In fact, some theoreticians started to doubt the validity of the previously iron-clad Efficient Market Hypothesis itself. Patterson continues:[21]

"The now-you-see-it-now-you-don't math wizards had a unique retort: Black Monday never happened. Jens Carten Jackwerth, a postdoctoral visiting scholar at the University of California at Berkeley, and Mark Rubinstein, coinventor of portfolio insurance, offered incontrovertible proof that October, 19, 1987 was statistically impossible. According to their probability formula, published in 1995, the likelihood of the crash was a "27-standard-deviation event," with a probability of 10 to the 160th power: <u>Even if one were to have lived through the entire 20 billion year life of the universe and experienced this 20 billion times (20 billion big bangs), that such a decline could have happened even once in this period is a virtual impossibility"</u>

Black Monday also represented a fascinating case study in the devastating effects of derivatives on financial markets. The Index Arbitrageurs, buying the S&P 500 futures being sold by portfolio insurance, had raced to short sell the underlying stock to stay net neutral. This was because by owning the S&P 500 futures, they effectively owned a small piece of every stock in the index. To hedge, they had to quickly short the underlying, so that any large loss in the index futures they owned would be offset by a gain on a short position in the individual stocks. However, the S&P 500 index itself was calculated based on the prices of the underlying securities. Thus, after portfolio insurance sold the arbs futures, the Index arbs short sold billions of dollars worth of stock, the S&P future market tanked, and LOR, seeing the massive volatility and downward pressure on the market, sold more and more futures, which caused the Arbs to short more and more stock. This was the unwelcome discovery of a vicious positive feedback loop, a "shadow risk" that existed beneath the surface of the market, unbeknownst to the very investors who traded in it. The Ouroboros had been awakened. These feedback loops, once initiated, continued until the underlying factors have been exhausted or until the agents in the system are self-destroyed.

Derivatives and the Alchemy of Risk

Derivatives are financial contracts that derive their value from an underlying security and have existed for as long as markets have. A futures contract, for example, is a legal agreement to buy or sell a particular commodity asset, or security at a predetermined price at a specified time in the future. The buyer of a futures contract is taking on the obligation to buy and receive the underlying asset when the futures contract expires, and the seller of the futures contract is taking on the obligation to deliver the underlying asset at the expiration date. These contracts have been around for millennia, with the earliest recorded contract dated to 1750 BC in Mesopotamia, or modern-day Iraq.

Say you're in a casino and you want to make money off a poker game, but you are barred from playing the actual game. So, you grab another patron (Dave) and tell him you'd like to make a bet on the outcome of the game. You really think your friend Allie will win the game, so you're willing to pony up $100 to bet on her winning. (In this analogy, the bet you make is the "derivative". The result of the first poker game is the performance of the underlying security). Seeing your derivative bet, two other people get interested. They don't want to bet on the game, rather they want to gamble on the outcome of your bet. They create their own bet, weighing probabilities and putting in funds accordingly. This is a second-order derivative. In the modern financial system, since derivatives are basically unregulated due to the Commodities Futures Modernization Act, (especially OTC derivatives or second-order or higher) this process can continue ad infinitum, with derivatives stacking on top of each other, each trying to mimic the underlying's returns.

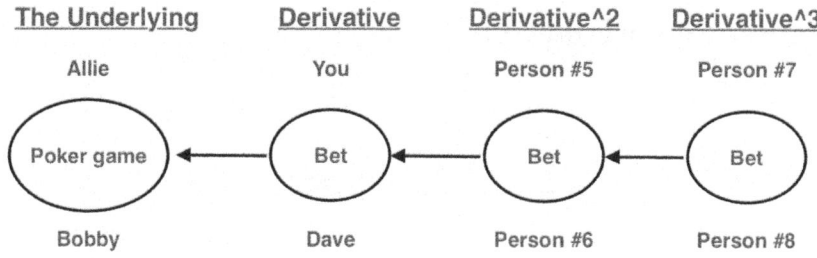

When putting together a collection of investments, many investors are concerned about potential losses. Investing in any individual stock is risky, so it's reasonable to try to minimize the potential for negative outcomes. This is one of the reasons why derivatives were developed. Hedging allows traders to transform their overall risk into a net risk. Net risk refers to the difference between a hedge fund's investments that are expected to increase in value and those that are expected to decrease in value. Once calculated, the net risk of a fund is often shown as a percentage, which illustrates how much market fluctuations could impact the fund's performance.

Let's break it down- say you are bullish on IBM. You go out and buy $50M of long dated call options (commonly called LEAPS) on IBM. Since you're afraid of losing money in case IBM misses its earnings call, loses revenue, or experiences some other negative event while your position is open, you go and buy $40M of put options with the same expiry date. Thus, your new net exposure position is only $10M long.

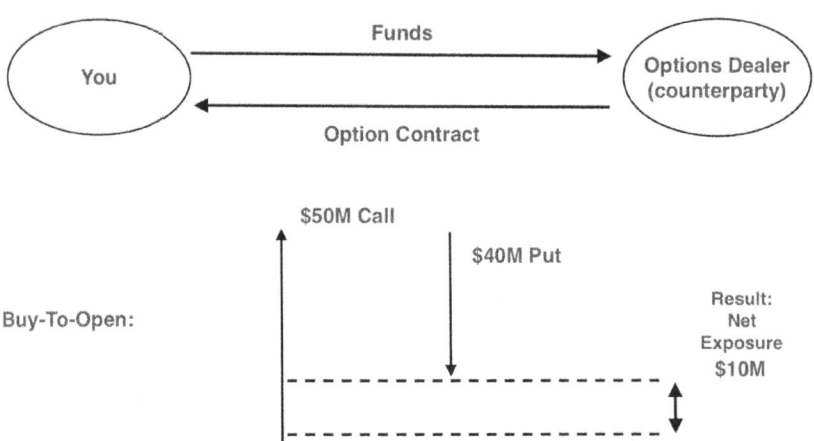

Using this mechanism, traders were able to hedge positions and reduce their theoretical risk. When you buy calls and puts, this net exposure is reduced, and at the same time, your assets increase. In the example above, your gross exposure (the gross value of the derivatives you own) will increase as you own both long calls and long puts.

Don't get this confused with being long/short or bullish/bearish a stock!! Long position for derivatives simply means you own the contract; short position means you owe the contract. "Long/ Short" is a general term in finance that can mean different things depending on the context.

Since both these calls and puts have value that you paid for, and represent the right to exercise at strike, they are both recorded as assets on your balance sheet. In the example above, you own $50M of calls and $40M of puts- your overall derivative gross exposure is $90M. Your net exposure is only $10M. Thus, you have $90M of assets (subject to market changes of course) and "net risk" of $10M.

There's three interrelated ways this goes seriously wrong. One is counterparty risk. A counterparty is someone who takes the opposite side of your trade- so if you are buying, they are the seller, and vice-versa. In derivatives, if the counterparty to your trade fails, i.e., goes bankrupt, the contract will most likely not be honored. This means if you are a hedge fund, and you bought OTC options, your $90M of calls and puts, if they were written with a single counterparty (like Bear Stearns) will now be worth NOTHING.

This $90M "gross exposure" loss would represent an 800%

higher loss than the "theoretical" maximum loss of $10M which is your "net exposure". If an options clearinghouse which is the counterparty to all listed options fails, millions of contracts would be worthless. The true risk is counterparty risk- this is what the models don't understand.

Another way this goes wrong is if the underlying fails- the results are equally catastrophic. Going back to the poker game analogy, imagine if the people playing the actual poker game left the table. Now derivative bet #1 is worthless, since there's nothing to bet on. Same goes with derivative bet #2, and #3, and so on. If the Poker game had $25 in the pot, and each derivative bet had $100 in each bet, this means that by the poker game ending, $325 worth of value was destroyed, from the elimination of just one real game worth $25. THIS is the explosive nature of derivatives.

Let's use the 2008 financial crisis as an example of an underlying security failure. A homeowner goes out and gets a loan (original poker game). The bank then sells that loan to an investment bank who makes a CDO out of it (a bet on the game) which trades on the value of the underlying. Then, another bank comes along and makes a synthetic CDO (a bet on the bet), and then takes out a credit default swap on it (bet on a bet on a bet). This creates insane leverage to the underlying, and horribly dangerous results if the underlying collapses. Dr. Susanne Trimbath puts it like this in her book Naked, Short and Greedy:[22]

"I've tried to say this in different ways to make it as clear as possible and I think the best way to look at it is to recognize that the problem that you see and talk about on the equity side, is multiplied 100 times in the bond markets and then another 15 times through credit default swaps. Basically, for every $1 in real value that any company or country puts into the financial markets, brokers are ramping it up and trading something like 1,875% of it. <u>Another way to look at it is that if a homeowner defaults on a $100,000 mortgage, it can do $187,500,000 worth of damage to financial markets.</u>"

A third way this system can blow up is due to cross-collateralization, where one asset is pledged to multiple entities, creating more claims than assets that exist. This process is actually very common in the futures markets- bullion banks, for example, which hold gold and silver, will write between 2-10 futures contracts for every one ounce of gold in the vaults.

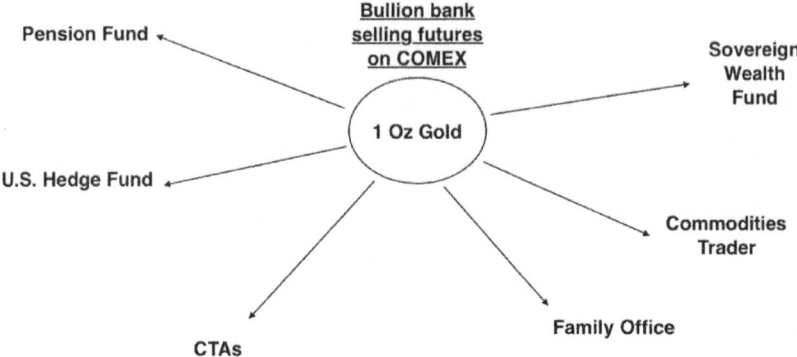

In the example above, the bullion bank (with the gold) writes 6 futures contracts (assume 1 ounce per contract) and sells them to other financial institutions, but only has a single ounce of gold in the vault. They can do this since the vast majority of the futures (~85-90%) never get called in for physical settlement, and are instead rolled forward (this basically means when the old contract is about to expire, the holder sells it for cash, and then uses this money to buy a new futures contract with a different expiration date).

Thus, the bank/institution writing all these futures never has to actually deliver the underlying- the gold in this case. If all the futures contracts they write are called in at once, then the 1 ounce of gold is given to the buyer, and the bank who wrote the contract is on the hook to deliver all 5 ounces to the firms that are owed, and is forced to go into the market to purchase it- this is called a "contract delivery squeeze" as outlined in a research paper published by the City University of New York.[23] If the bullion bank fails, all the futures written by it are now null and void, and the firms that couldn't take delivery get nothing.

The Market Value is the value of the derivative at its current trading price. The Notional Value is the value of the derivative if it was at its strike price.

E.g., A call option represents 100 shares of ABC stock with a strike of $50. Perhaps it is trading in the market at $1 per contract right now.

Market Value= 100 shares * $1 per contract = $100

Notional Value= 100 shares* $50 strike price= $5,000

The notional value is the true value of total liabilities within the derivatives market, although this is misleading since the likelihood of all derivatives reaching notional value is exceedingly low.

Systemic Risk

The recent Archegos Capital debacle was a classic example of the destructive power of derivatives. Using contracts like total return swaps, Bill Hwang was able to leverage his fund more than 8x, making bets on the performance of a variety of Chinese and American equities. When the equities lost value, his fund was obliterated- a mere 12.5% drop in the underlying resulted in a complete loss of capital. But his fund wasn't the only firm affected- Credit Suisse was his counterparty, and thus lost more than $5.5 Billion, and counting. If derivatives are an explosive bottle, counterparty risk is a fuse- one that always runs to another bottle of nitroglycerin.

The modern financial system is effectively a complex network of institutions, tied to each other through these complex derivative contracts. GSIBs (Globally Systemic Important Banks) are the largest entities in the system, tied directly to thousands of institutions, and indirectly to hundreds of thousands.

The entire derivatives market is gargantuan. The BIS estimated the total notional value of the OTC derivatives market to be $640 Trillion in 2019[24]! And that doesn't even include exchange-listed derivatives like most common option contracts. More sober estimates put it somewhere north of $1 quadrillion. Numbers of this size are hard to wrap your head around- this is equivalent to a million billion, or a thousand trillion- for reference, the U.S. economy is around $22 trillion, and the world economy is estimated to be $88 trillion- thus the entire world economy could fit into the notional derivatives market 11x over and still not reach it. Every single bank is exposed, either directly or indirectly, to this market. For example, Deutsche Bank alone has over $47 Trillion in notional gross exposure- twice the size of the entire US Economy![25]

Through the magic of financial engineering, Deutsche is able to create a net exposure of only $22 billion, equivalent to 0.046% of the notional. Thus, although on paper the net risk is extremely small, the actual risk to the firm is enough to wipe it out overnight. This is what happened to institutions like AIG in the 2008 crisis - they insured more products than they could ever cover, and when the firms they insured came calling they were quickly forced into bankruptcy, requiring a $182 billion bailout from the Federal Reserve.

If the hedge funds with derivatives exposure (like Archegos) are the equivalent of an office rigged with nitroglycerin, the banks are stadiums full of 50 gallon drums- and the DTCC/ICC/OCC are the equivalent of a nuke. Counterparty risk, in the form of fuses, runs between all of them. What happens when enough factors on the system start to apply too much pressure? BOOM.

Why hasn't anything happened? This is the question most people ask themselves when they first learn about this. The reason is actually very simple. As long as money keeps flowing into the casino, the gamblers feel little risk, so no one pulls out. The Fed continues to print money, equity/bond prices continue to rise, and since there's "no risk" of the underlying falling in value, everyone keeps their money in the pot, and the poker game continues. The profits made from derivatives trading are enormous, and any bank that stopped doing this would quickly lose investors, because they would instantly take their capital out and take it to another bank that actually is profitable. It's all a confidence game- as long as everyone keeps trusting the system, prices keep rising, and the cash keeps pumping in, the party will continue.

Warren Buffet famously turned down calls to buy Lehman Brothers during the darkest days of the financial crisis- he understood a key concept, that derivatives are financial weapons of mass destruction, able to destroy entire firms, and indeed entire banking systems, in one fell swoop.

In the tumultuous month of October 2008, this system was beginning to unravel. The money draining out of the financial system due to bank runs and frozen credit lending started to light fires in multiple financial institutions. The bombs that were Bear Sterns, AIG and Lehman had already blown up, and the fire was spreading through counterparty risk throughout the system. In fact, we were getting dangerously close to hitting the switch on the nuclear warhead- As Timothy Geitner (Pres of New York Fed) put it, "We were a few days away from the ATMs not working"[26]

And the worst part of all of this? Even to this day, regulators, and indeed even financial industry insiders, are completely blind to the risk. OTC derivatives are essentially unregulated- no one knows the true size of this market. Worse yet, the traders inside the bank are using optimistic versions of the Efficient Market Hypothesis and VaR models to estimate their risk, which comes out to essentially 0 due to the risk models and net exposure hedging. Thus, they pile on more risk every day, ensuring that this problem continues to grow until the entire system explodes.

The modern international financial system, unhinged from the fetters of regulation and oversight, has created a derivatives monster whose tendrils reach across the globe. Nourished by the incessant money printer and holding the retirement funds of generations, this machine continues to bet, in ever-increasing amounts, in the greatest casino ever created. This monster, as long as it is nourished by cheap credit and ever-increasing flows of cash from the Federal Reserve, will continue to grow. This is why the Fed is in the endgame- they know that they cannot turn off the liquidity hose, as they would risk destroying the system in its entirety. They have to convince themselves and the market with constant assurances that inflation will remain low, risk is non-existent, and their balance sheet can continue to grow without consequence. Secretly, they are starting to realize they are trapped in a burning building with no way out.

THE MONEY MACHINE

Debt Cycles and the Impossible Object

"T he global financial markets walk on the razor's edge between empiricism and what you see is not what you think. The Impossible Object in art is an illustration that highlights the limitations of human perception and is an appropriate construct for our modern capitalist dystopia. The fundamental characteristic of the impossible object is uncertainty of perception. Is it feasible for a real waterfall to flow into itself; or a triangle to twist itself in both directions?

Modern financial markets are a game of impossible objects. In a world where global central banks manipulate the cost of risk, the mechanics of price discovery have disengaged from reality resulting in paradoxical expressions of value that should not exist according to efficient market theory. Fear and safety are now interchangeable in a speculative and high stakes game of perception. **What you see is not what exists, and what exists cannot be understood**"[27]

Banking and Debt Cycles

The modern banking system can trace its origins to the early days of the Renaissance, in Northern Italy. There, in affluent trading cities such as Florence, Venice, and Genoa, traders dealing solely in finance would set up a bench (called banca in Old Italian- where the modern word bank comes from) financing voyages, engaging in arbitrage, and funding shipbuilding for merchants. Banks of that period dealt almost exclusively in gold and silver coins and traded these coins freely for foreign coins stamped by a different king. They quickly realized that dealing in physical coins was costly, burdensome, and dangerous, as thieves would often rob money-laden wagons traveling between towns.

So, they came up with an innovative solution. Instead of handing over coins to their customers, they would ask that the customer place their gold or silver in the bank's vault, which already stored the bank's own money, and in return the bank would hand them a banknote, or a physical receipt of ownership of the gold. The customer could then take this note and pay for real goods or services someplace else instead of carrying the coins.

The banks quickly saw a loophole- no one was auditing their vaults and comparing how much gold was there versus how many notes the bank had issued. The financiers over time began to issue more notes than gold in the vault[28]. This system would work fine as long as every customer had confidence in their banknote and believed that the gold backing their coins was actually there.

However, once the bank started facing financial troubles, and customers showed up to redeem their notes for gold, a bank run would immediately begin. The end result was often many clients ending up with worthless pieces of paper after the vaults were emptied. Authorities created extreme punishments for bankers caught issuing more notes than gold in the vault - in some places in Medieval Italy, death penalties were enforced for bankers caught issuing too many notes- in others, life in prison was the punishment.

Our modern financial system is based on the early Italian antecedents. Most people believe that when you deposit funds into the bank, the money stays in your account. In reality, the funds you invest are immediately lent out, re-deposited, and lent out again. This is called fractional reserve banking. Thus, the "money" you see in your bank account is a lie. It isn't really there.

Let's break down how this works. Say you earn $1000 from a recent paycheck. You go to your bank and deposit these funds. The next day, the bank takes $900 (90%) of the cash you deposited and loans it out, keeping 10% in reserve in case you come to withdraw some of it.

This money is given to person #1, who takes this loan and buys some paint for his house. The vendor who sold him the paint then takes the $900 received and deposits it in the bank. The bank then repeats the process, loaning out 90% of the money, or $810 to person #3, who spends/invests it with person #4, who deposits it again, and the process repeats. Here it is visualized:

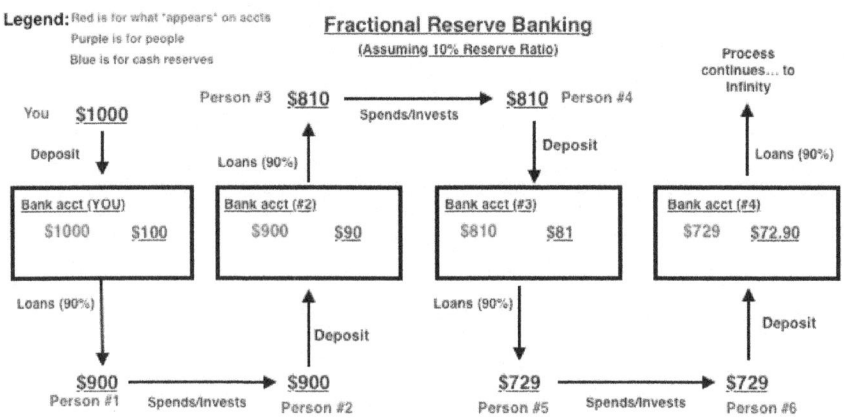

All along the way, the bank is able to basically loan money into existence, and charge interest on the loans it creates. This is essentially a near- infinite money glitch in the system and allows banks to make exorbitant profits. However, this process also serves to greatly increase systemic risk- in the example above, one single $1000 transaction is turned into what appears as $3,439 in bank accounts, but is actually just credit, re-deposited and re-borrowed over and over again.

In a 21st century digitized economy, very few people even use cash so banks are not required to keep that much cash on hand to honor redemptions. Most "money" that exists only lives on an internal SQL ledger, and these ledgers are settled against each other through the interbank settlement systems. Each bank also has an account at the Fed, where it stores bank reserves.

In the modern iteration of fractional reserve banking, there is basically no limit to loans receivable for a bank to create except for economic demand. This is part of the reason why low interest rates are so beneficial to financial institutions, as it increases demand for debt and thus allows them to loan more money into existence. Since March 15th, 2020, the Federal Reserve has established that bank capital requirements are zero percent. There is no need any longer for any type of cash or deposit to back a loan and banks can lend freely.

Typically, the majority of a banks' capital provided to

businesses will be business loans, lines of credit, or venture financing. These business loans will be put to work to expand factories, build new products, hire workers, or create intellectual property- generally things that expand economic growth. This effectively means that the vast majority of what we "think" of as money, is not cash, but credit.[29] Most funds in the system, thus, exist in the form of debt- 94% credit, and 6% cash, to be exact.

Another effect of fractional reserve banking is a supercharging of the debt cycle. Because banks are allowed to loan money into existence, banks are able to create massive amounts of credit, helping to boost economic growth in the boom stage, and worsen economic decline in a bust. The debt cycle is an economic phenomenon that has been observed for centuries- in ancient Israel, for example, the state enforced a debt "jubilee" every fifty years (a long human lifespan) to dissolve all debts, release people from bondage, and restore ancestral lands to the descendants.

There are two main cycles- the long term "super" cycle, which lasts between 50-80 years (longer in countries with higher life expectancy, so most developed countries this is 80 years) and the short term "normal" cycle, which occurs every 8-10 years or so. The credit cycle undergoes both expansionary and contractionary phases. Let's look at the four phases of a typical credit cycle.

1. Expansion: During periods of strong economic activity, corporate cash flows tend to improve as consumer confidence rises, and financial institutions increase their lending efforts. In this environment, businesses have easier access to capital markets, which can facilitate growth and allow enterprises to take on more financial leverage.
2. Downturn: A downturn in the credit cycle is usually the result of an economic slowdown or the possibility of a recession, which leads to stricter credit standards. This downturn often follows a period of peak business expansion and high financial leverage, and the resulting slowdown in business growth and decline in earnings can lead to potential defaults.
3. Repair: After a downturn in the credit cycle, the repair phase occurs as the economy begins to recover. During this time, companies may focus on improving their financial stability by reducing costs and decreasing financial leverage. This is meant to strengthen their balance sheets and prepare them for future growth.
4. Recovery: During the recovery phase, confidence begins to improve as corporate balance sheets become stronger due to relatively low financial leverage. Financial institutions may also begin to relax their lending standards at this time. This phase marks the return to more stable economic conditions and the start of a new credit cycle.

The Great Depression

The previous debt super cycle reached its peak in the 1930s.

The United States was showing signs of economic recovery after the stock market crash of 1929, but a series of bank panics in late 1930 led to the start of the Great Depression instead. This event marked the beginning of a prolonged period of economic downturn and hardship. At the beginning of the crisis, there were over 8,000 commercial banks that were members of the Federal Reserve System, but nearly 16,000 that were not. These nonmember banks operated in a similar environment to the one that existed prior to the establishment of the Federal Reserve in 1914, which was prone to banking crises.

One reason for the financial crisis in 1930 was the inclusion of "floating" checks, or checks that were still being collected, in a bank's cash reserves. These checks were counted as reserves at both the bank where they were deposited and the bank on which they were drawn, even though the funds were only physically present at one of the institutions. This practice was known as "fictitious reserves" by bankers of the time. The quantity of fictitious reserves increased significantly during the 1920s and reached its highest point just prior to the crisis. This meant that the entire banking system had a smaller amount of actual reserves available to rely on during times of crisis.

One issue during bank panics was the difficulty of accessing bank reserves. Nonmember banks typically kept some of their reserves in physical cash form in their vaults and the majority in deposits at "correspondent banks" in certain cities. Some, but not all, of these correspondent banks were part of the Federal Reserve System. This hierarchical reserve structure made it difficult for rural banks to access reserves during emergencies. If a bank needed cash because its customers were withdrawing large amounts of money due to panic, the bank had to turn to its correspondent bank, which may have been dealing with requests from multiple other banks at the same time or could have been facing its own depositor runs.

On November 7, 1930, one of the main subsidiaries of Caldwell (a large financial conglomerate that had lost a significant amount of money through stock market speculation), the Bank of Tennessee, shut down. On November 12 and 17, Caldwell affiliates in Knoxville, Tennessee, and Louisville, Kentucky also collapsed. The failures of these banks caused a domino effect, leading many commercial banks to halt operations. In areas where these banks closed, depositors became panicked and withdrew large amounts of money from other banks. This panic spread quickly from one town to another. Within a few weeks, hundreds of banks had suspended operations. While about one-third of these banks were able to reopen within a few months, the majority were liquidated.[30] Businesses that relied on loan financing started to collapse, and unemployment started to climb.

What followed was a protracted period of bank runs and panics lasting for years. Contrary to common belief, not all bank runs happened at the same time- some banks experienced one or two runs- others more than that. The Great Depression was a series of panics, rather, that culminated in a near-complete collapse of the banking system and a ban on gold as legal tender by FDR in Executive Order 6102. In the wake of the crisis, several key financial reforms were made. Among them were the creation of FDIC (Federal Deposit Insurance Corporation) which was created in 1933 to "insure" bank deposits with government funds. This, it was hypothesized, would stop bank runs and restore confidence in the system. Another reform was the creation of the Glass - Steagall Act, a key legal provision that forced commercial and investment banks to remain separate entities.

However, both of these in time would serve to further increase risk, not reduce it. The FDIC, for example, insured $100k (later updated to $250K during 2008) of bank deposits. This was supposedly done for the benefit of the client, but many overlook that it also greatly benefited the bank. When you deposit cash into a bank, it is an asset to you- but to the bank, this is a liability- it represents a cash amount that they will have to pay out to you upon your request. By insuring the deposit, the bank gets essentially free insurance on their liabilities, which allows them to justify taking more leverage. Glass- Steagall's separation of banks was an amazing step at reforming the system- sadly, it was repealed in 1999 by Bill Clinton under the Gramm–Leach–Bliley Act (GLBA). Commercial banks are where you deposit funds, get mortgages, small business loans, and personal lines of credit; investment banks are firms that underwrite financial transactions, create derivatives, and speculate in the market. By combining the two, banks are essentially allowed to bet with depositors' money- and if they fail, they can rightly justify to regulators that their collapse would end in financial calamity for millions of working-class depositors who would lose everything since their accounts would be suspended. Thus, they have become "Too Big to Fail" institutions and receive federal government bailouts, no matter how fiscally reckless they have been.

The Money Illusion

In 2008, we were at the end of a major debt super cycle. The frenzied mortgage lending and securitization in the financial sector, along with massive consumer credit borrowing, had set the U.S. up for a major crisis. In relative terms, we were at a 27% higher total debt to GDP ratio than the Great Depression. These massive debt loads were coming home to roost, manifesting first as a crisis in subprime but then quickly moving to prime mortgages, corporate debt markets, money markets, and even the consumer credit markets. Panic began to spread about a new depressionary crisis forming on the economic horizon. Ben Bernanke, the Chairman of the Federal Reserve, was a self-avowed student of the Great Depression- and was determined not to let it happen again. He, along with Treasury Secretary Hank Paulson (Former CEO of Goldman Sachs) and Tim Geitner, created new lending facilities and MBS purchase programs in order to swallow the massive amounts of toxic assets the system had created.

Paulson and Bernanke technically had no legal authority to create these programs, but in a crisis, all caution goes out the window. TARP and other programs authorized by the Treasury bought billions of dollars of MBS, funded by T-bond issuances. This chart shows U.S. government debt as a % of GDP through today:[31] (notice the spike in debt during and after 2008)

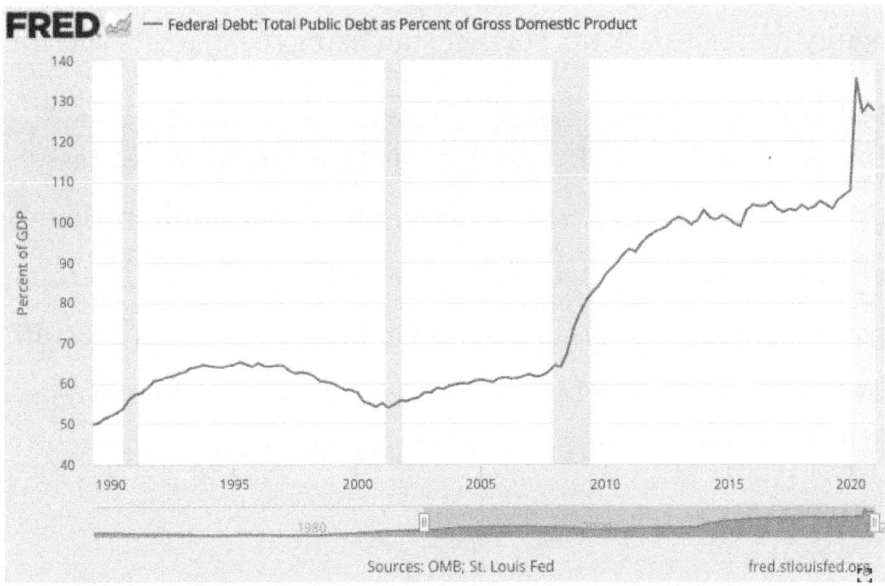

Sources: OMB; St. Louis Fed   fred.stlouisfed.org

The United States borrowed heavily- TARP alone was authorized for $700 billion. The Treasury did not have the funds to support this, so it issued billions of dollar's worth of bonds. Banks, hedge funds, other governments, and the Fed all bought this debt en masse. The primary dealers (banks approved to trade directly with the Treasury) buy government bonds from the U.S. Treasury and turn around and sell these bonds to the Fed or other third parties. The massive issuance of debt was swallowed wholesale by the financial system.

In the equity markets, as we started bottoming in the first quarter of 2009, hedge funds, banks, and family offices began loading up on margin debt again. This renewed confidence in the banking system and overall lending capacity began pushing equity markets back up. Further stabilizing the markets was the Federal Reserve with their massive quantitative easing program. In 2008, the Federal Reserve's balance sheet ballooned- assets grew from $880 billion pre-crisis, to $2 trillion immediately after, and eventually over $4 trillion by 2014. Many economists, particularly those with a libertarian bent, such as Peter Schiff, immediately decried this reckless behavior and predicted hyper-inflation as early as 2011. See the graph below for reference:[32]

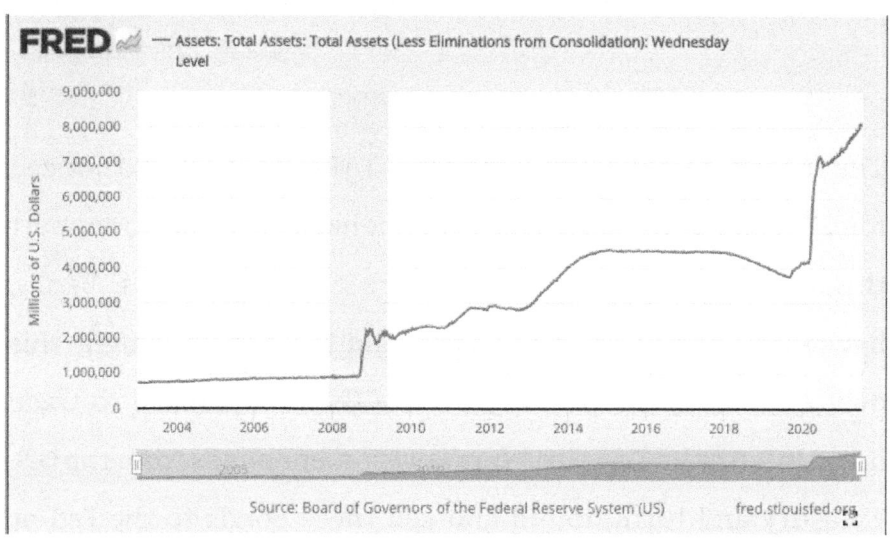

When the Fed buys assets, it is completely different from any other institution buying. Pension plans or mutual funds use the savings of the investors of the fund. Because that money came either from working, or from other investments, it represents no net increase in money supply. The money they received had to come from someone else, for a good/product/service/asset they created or provided. However, the Fed has no taxing authority, no savings, no funds to speak of at all- everything the Fed buys it purchases through money it prints. Thus, Fed balance sheet expansion equals money printing (at least in the form of bank reserves). The Fed printed $2 trillion in the two years following the fall of 2008.

This rampant money printing rightly worried experts and pundits in the media- but the inflation they feared never came. Why? Well, most of the new money that was printed went directly into the banking system. Lyn Alden describes it brilliantly:[33]

"Leading into the financial crisis, only about 13% of bank reserve assets consisted of cash (3%) and Treasury securities (10%). The rest of their assets were invested in loans and riskier securities. This was also at a time when household debt to GDP reached a record high, as consumers were caught up in the housing bubble. That over-leveraged bank situation hit a climax into the 2008/2009 crisis, coinciding with record high debt-to-GDP among households, and was the apex of the long-term private (non-federal) debt cycle. When banks are that leveraged with very little cash reserves, even a 3% loss in assets results in insolvency. And that's what happened; the banking system as a whole hit a peak total loan charge-off rate of over 3%, and it resulted in a widespread banking crisis."

Thus, the new money went to recapitalize banks and shore up their balance sheets to defend them from bankruptcy- it stayed in untouchable bank reserves, and never entered circulation. The money that didn't go to repair bank balance sheets flowed directly into the equity and bond indexes. Overall, there are two different economies- the real economy, and the financial economy. The tidal wave of new money the Fed was creating did not cause inflation (in the traditional sense), because the money did not flow into the real economy- the goods, products and services that everyone consumes daily. The money instead flowed into the financial economy- bond markets, stock markets, private equity funds, commodities, Forex markets, etc.

When you give a bank $100M, it doesn't go out and buy $100M worth of Big Macs and Kleenex- the bank puts these funds into investments, generally either in the form of loans or in the form of equities or equity derivatives. "Wait a second!"- you say. "The Fed printed money to buy treasury bonds, and the Treasury usually spends funds that go into the real economy, so that should have caused inflation, right?"

Yes, this is typically what happens. But, during and after the 2008 financial crisis the majority of new Treasury expenditures went to programs that were stabilizing the financial system

(TARP+ TAF+ TLGP+ others). So, a large portion of the money that would have been spent by government agencies in the real economy instead just flowed back to banks and financial institutions.[34]

Typically, in a recession the Treasury will increase spending to cushion the blow to workers- and in 2009 they did extend a few unemployment benefits. But, by and large, Congress authorized few benefit programs for workers, and the average time on the benefit decreased after a slight bump in 2009. Thus, the amount of freshly printed money that reached the real economy was minimal, and whatever money did reach it largely acted to counteract deflationary forces. It wasn't enough to actually induce inflation. The government did little to stop foreclosures or provide aid to small businesses. Unemployment spiked, and due to the Phillips Curve principle discussed earlier there was a dampening effect on inflation.

The funds the Federal Reserve had created, therefore, created no inflation in the real economy- instead they flowed to the financial economy and began to inflate assets. This started off the largest and longest bull market run in American stock market history- easily beating emerging and other developed countries' equity markets. Keynesian economists lauded this as an accomplishment- they believed they were creating what is called a "wealth effect" - a theory that stated that as people's financial wealth increased, they would be induced to do more spending and investment- thus, by propping up the stock market, they would stimulate the real economy. This is awfully convenient for the rich- the top 10% own 85% of the equity markets, and thus have seen their wealth balloon by over 186% while growth for everyone else stagnated.[35]

Ironically this theory has it exactly backwards- real economic growth should drive the stock market, not the other way around. But, convinced of their theories, economic policymakers continued to pump ever increasing sums into the financial system. The entire "rally" we have experienced for the past 12 years has been nothing but an illusion- it is simply the result of vast money inflows into the financial system. Banks and financial institutions will do everything they can to convince you that the high stock market valuations are justified by fundamental growth. This is wrong- these valuations are not justified. Insane levels of money printing and debt leverage have created extremely dislocated equity markets. For example, Square (SQ) as of August 2021 has a forward PE ratio of 499.87- it currently doesn't pay a dividend, but let's assume it paid a 3% dividend payout ratio (which is rare for tech stocks) - if that were the case, it would take 14,996 years for the dividends to pay back the price of a single share.

The markets are slowly being "walked up" every day that QE continues. Throughout 2021, the ultimate price insensitive buyer (the Fed) is plowing $120 billion a month into Treasuries and MBS, and the primary dealers now must turn around and put their money somewhere. The bond market is already a trap with 2% yields, and 5% inflation, thus there is little profit potential there, so these institutions are forced to buy equities if they want any returns. The Fed is killing whatever is left of price discovery. Four billion dollars or so a day is being pumped into the system- and going straight to the markets.

Further, to stimulate growth in the real economy, policymakers during the last decade or so dropped interest rates to near 0% to induce bank lending to get consumers to borrow and spend again. Approximately 70% of our economy is consumption.[36]

This did create massive loan demand- basically every sector of the U.S. economy began borrowing en masse. The Fed was able to "reinflate" the bubble and allow the economy to survive on debt financing to "re-invigorate the economy". Fast-forward to July 2021, and a decade of pinning rates to the zero-bound has us breaking records in terms of debt loads:

Student Loan Debt: at $1.7 Trillion.[37]

Corporate Debt: at 46.4% of GDP, highest ever.[38]

Consumer Credit Card Debt hit 21% of GDP, a record high.[39]

Auto Loan Debt at $1.4 Trillion, an all-time high.[40]

I could go on and on, but you get the point. Now, the entire system is overleveraged- the cancer has spread, and it has infected virtually every single sector of the economy.

People keep saying that we "kicked the can" of 2008 down the road. This is wrong. We kicked the can up the stairs- meaning, we not only delayed the problem, but made sure it would get worse, since we borrowed more to paper over the old debts and worthless securities the system had created. A fascinating aspect of our recent financial history is that the bailouts are exponentially growing- this is due to the simple fact that the entity giving the bailout has to have a balance sheet multiples larger than the firm receiving the bailout, and government guarantees of banks induce reckless speculation. For example, to bailout a bank with $10B in mark-to-market losses, you need a bank with a $20 or $30B capital surplus, to absorb the loss and keep the depositors and creditors satisfied that the bank giving the bailout won't go under. In 1998, a hedge fund called LTCM was near collapse- it had leveraged itself over 25-1, using complex algorithms made by Nobel Prize winning economists to predict bond prices. They had made massive derivative bets buying Russian bonds (among other things) - and when the Russian government defaulted in August 1998, their positions began to unravel. The massive debt and derivative exposure they had created was threatening to pull several large banks down with it. The Fed stepped in during September of that year to organize a $3.5 billion bailout, funded by 12 large banks.[41] According to James Rickards, general counsel of LTCM - the U.S. equity and bond markets were close to being completely shut off during the worst of that crisis.

In 2008, the entire U.S. financial system was nearing collapse and desperately needed a bailout. A massive bank run had begun. Congress stepped up and provided- in the end spending over $498 billion of taxpayer funds.[42] However, the Fed also provided a bailout (though QE), eventually buying over $1.7 trillion of mortgage backed securities. Since the Great Financial Crisis, the banking system debt crisis has now become a government debt crisis, and indeed an economic debt crisis- and this debt has spread worldwide. Equity and bond markets have continued to march up, despite fundamental factors worsening. This new financial paradigm was rightly termed "The Everything Bubble". Total (govt+private) global debt now stands at a staggering 356% of GDP.[43] We've never been here before- we are now navigating uncharted waters. The next bailout will have to be bigger- a LOT bigger.

The financial crisis was the beginning of a debt avalanche- it's likely that around half of the major banks, mortgage brokers, and other financial institutions would have gone bankrupt, superseding the Great Depression-era record of 30%. Thousands of private and public companies would have gone bankrupt. Real estate and equity markets would have entered a freefall lasting for years, and unemployment would likely have spiked past 30%, bringing back the soup lines not seen since 1936. Instead, policymakers kicked the can up the stairs- they issued massive amounts of government debt to paper over the 2008 crisis, and incentivized excessive borrowing in the private sector. The fundamental factors that caused the crisis (unregulated derivatives, excessive leverage, lack of oversight) were never resolved. As Criand so elegantly puts it, "2008 never ended". Now, with federal debt standing at over $31 trillion, there are only tough choices ahead. We will soon reach a point where the interest payments alone on the debt supersede all U.S. tax revenues- when that happens, we will have traveled beyond the event horizon- there will be no coming back. The debt will be impossible to pay off. This is according to the government's own projections, per the CBO chart below.[44]

Figure 1.

Federal Debt Held by the Public, 1900 to 2050

Percentage of Gross Domestic Product

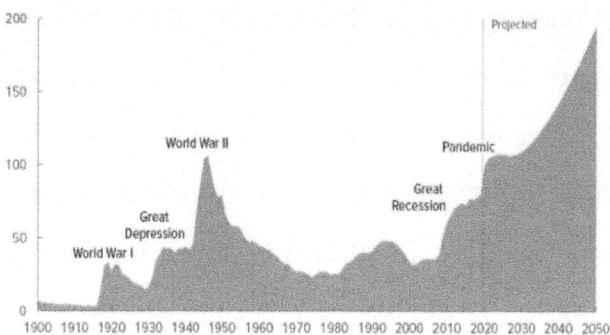

Growing deficits are projected to drive federal debt held by the public to unprecedented levels over the next 30 years. By 2050, debt is projected to reach 195 percent of gross domestic product.

Source: Congressional Budget Office.

The United States continues to borrow- running a staggering $2.1 trillion deficits for just the first half of 2021.[45] Day by day, we are adding snow to the mountains above our village. When this will end is anyone's guess but borrowing more will only make the end worse. The debt crisis will return, but this time, it will be the financial system, U.S. government, and indeed the entire world economy that needs a bailout- and who has a big enough balance sheet to absorb that?

The only answer is the ones with an infinite balance sheet- the central banks.

The idea that anyone can borrow forever, or print money forever, with no consequences, defies basic financial logic. Impossible objects cannot exist forever. History shows deadly consequences for the nations that venture down either path. The United States is no exception.

The Fed has already tried to escape this trap in 2018. It failed. Sovereign creditors are losing faith in the U.S. Treasury and have been since 2015. The walls are closing in, and the ultimate decision must be made. The avalanche is coming either way- and we only have two choices. Either we allow ourselves to be buried under a mountain of hyper-deflation, creating a new Great Depression, frozen credit and equity markets, and massive bank failures or we burn our way out, using the inferno of money printing and hyper-inflation.

FINANCIAL GRAVITY

The Fed's Dilemma

The Federal Reserve is now trapped in a black hole of its own design. Continually crushed by the weight of the financial debt, the economy and markets themselves keep contracting inwards towards collapse. 2008 was a foreshadowing of what was to come- and in 2018, the system was beginning to unravel again. The Fed, desperate to prevent this, persists in heaping more and more liquidity and debt onto the system, desperately praying that there will be a way out. Their monetary tools are self-defeating; paradoxically, they serve to make the problems worse instead of addressing the root issues. QE can warp the fabric of space-time to a certain extent, ripping markets higher, distorting price discovery, and supercharging the debt cycle; it cannot, however, create actual economic growth. This requires real work.

What they fail to understand is that they have already crossed the event horizon; there is no escape. The Fed is on a collision course with Einsteinian physics; soon they will have to make a fatal choice of which to save- financial economy or real, markets or the Fed's credibility, the financial system or the dollar itself.

In the cold darkness of space no one can hear you scream.

The Panic of 1907 and the Creature from Jekyll Island

During the post-Civil War period of industrial growth, the deficiencies of the United States' fractional reserve banking system became increasingly prominent. These banks often experienced "runs" or panics due to insufficient cash reserves to meet the demands of customers during times of economic stress, resulting in numerous banks being forced to close. If a bank experienced a shortage of cash, it could cause panic at other financial institutions as customers sought to withdraw their funds before their own bank failed. If many banks were unable to fulfill these sudden demands for cash, it could lead to a domino effect of bank failures. In 1907, a particularly severe bank panic ended only when J.P. Morgan, a wealthy financier, used his personal resources to provide emergency loans to struggling banks.

The Panic of 1907 began in October 1907 and lasted for six weeks. Prior to the Panic, the U.S. Treasury, under the leadership of Secretary Leslie Shaw, engaged in significant purchases of government bonds and removed the requirement for banks to hold reserves against government deposits. This fueled an increase in the money supply and credit availability across the country, as well as an increase in stock market speculation, which ultimately contributed to the Panic of 1907. The bank panic was significantly influenced by the involvement of trust companies in New York City. These trust companies were state-chartered financial intermediaries that competed with other financial institutions. However, trusts were not central to the settlement system and also had a lower volume of check clearing compared to banks.

As a result of their low volume of check clearing, trust companies typically had a lower cash-to-deposit ratio compared to national banks. On average, trusts would hold about 5% cash in relation to deposits, while national banks held about 25% in reserve. Trust companies were vulnerable to runs on deposits, just like other financial institutions, because the demand deposits at trusts were payable in cash.

The Panic of 1907 was initially sparked by the bankruptcy of two small brokerage firms. The failed attempt by speculators Fritz Augustus Heinze and Charles W. Morse to acquire a large number of shares in a copper mining company, using significant margin loans, led to a run on investment banks that had financed their attempt to manipulate the copper market. The panic was exacerbated by a loss of confidence in trust companies, even as the situation at banks improved. One of the most notable trust companies to fail was Knickerbocker Trust, which had previously worked with Heinze.

Knickerbocker, the third-largest trust company in New York City, was denied a loan by J.P. Morgan and was unable to withstand the high volume of redemption requests. It eventually failed in late October. The failure of Knickerbocker Trust and other trust companies further eroded the public's trust in the financial sector, leading to an intensification of bank runs. The Panic of 1907 initially affected New York City, but eventually spread to other economic centers in the United States. In many ways, this crisis was reminiscent of the 2008 financial crisis, which was also characterized by overleveraged institutions, financial speculation, and shadow banks.

In an effort to prevent the cascading failures of banks, Morgan, Rockefeller, and newly-appointed Treasury Secretary George Cortelyou provided liquidity in the form of loans and bank deposits worth tens of millions of dollars to several New York banks and trusts. In the days following the Panic of 1907, J.P. Morgan pressured New York banks to provide loans to stock brokerages in order to maintain liquidity in the stock market and prevent the closure of the New York Stock Exchange. Morgan also arranged for the acquisition of the Tennessee Coal, Iron, and Railroad Company (TC&I) by U.S. Steel, which he owned, in order to bail out one of the largest brokerages that had borrowed heavily using TC&I stock as collateral.

A spike in the interest rate on overnight collateral loans, provided by the NYSE, was one of the first signals that trouble was brewing. Annualized loan rates ripped upwards from 9.5% to a whopping 70% on the very same day that the Knickerbocker shut down. Two days later, it was at 100%. J.P. Morgan was able to secure the continued operation of the NYSE by obtaining funds from influential financial organizations and major industries, which he subsequently made available to brokers willing to take on loans. After a delay of several days, the New York Clearing House Committee assembled a panel to advocate for the insurance of clearinghouse loan certificates. This action provided a temporary increase in liquidity and was a precursor to the window loans later offered by the Federal Reserve.

The 1907 financial crisis spurred a push for reform. Some Americans believed that a central bank was necessary to regulate the money supply and offer a flexible currency that could adjust to changes in the economy's need for money and credit. Others opposed this idea, viewing it as an attempt to continually bail out failing banks. As bankers grew concerned about future financial crises without a figure like

J.P. Morgan to rely on, they began to advocate for Congress to create a permanent solution to bank runs. After several years of negotiation, Congress ultimately established the Federal Reserve System on December 23, 1913.

Under a fractional reserve banking system, no bank has enough cash on hand to give out during redemptions. Money deposited in a bank account is very quickly lent out again, with only a fraction (say 10%) being kept on hand to handle withdrawals. As a run on one bank would ensue, the web of financial obligations that tied the banks together would start pulling other banks down with it. Any loans owed by the bank in crisis would immediately start to be downgraded, and the creditor banks, even if healthy, would see the value of their assets fall as the market started pricing in the default of the collapsing bank. What was seen in the crisis of 1907 was not only a credit collapse, but a collapse of confidence- the entire banking system was thrown into question, as depositors did not know which bank was solvent and which was not. Similar to the Prisoner's Dilemma, individual depositors, knowing even though leaving the money in the banks would make the system as a whole much safer, took the conservative route and pulled as much money out as they could. What the banks needed at this time were cash loans- but at the very moment they most desperately needed it, the loans were not available as other banks faced runs as well.

Thus, the Fed was created as a "Lender of Last Resort"- it could create bank reserves out of thin air and lend them to banks in order to ensure their solvency.

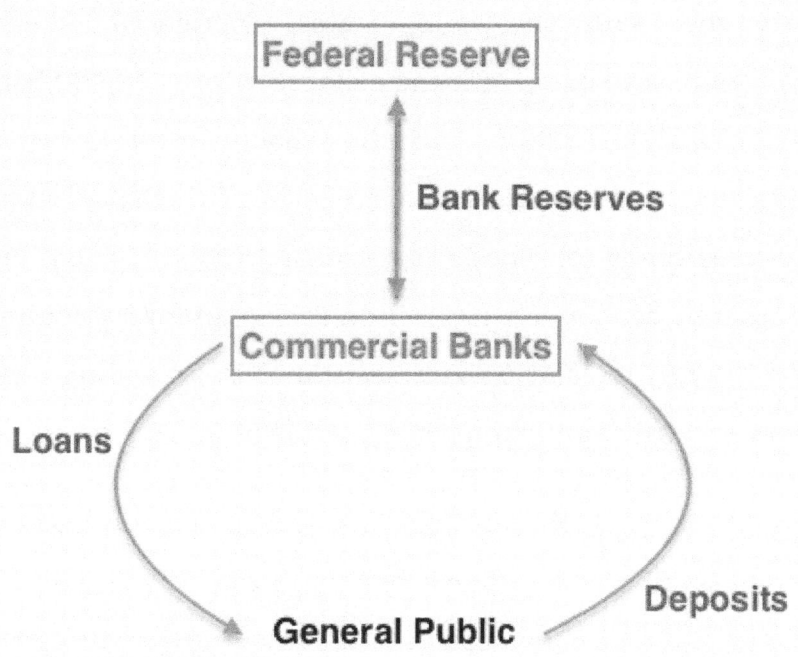

Many were infuriated by the creation of the Federal Reserve, which they viewed as a perpetual savior to Wall Street and a breeding ground for "moral hazard", an economics term used to describe a situation that occurs when an entity has an incentive to increase its exposure to risk because it does not bear the full costs of that risk. For example, when a corporation is insured, it may take on higher risk knowing that its insurance will pay the associated costs. With time, their predictions would prove to be correct. With every financial crisis, the Fed's power has grown, so much so that the institution would not be recognizable today to those who first founded it in the winter of 1913.

During the 1930s, the United States experienced its worst banking crisis to date, with the collapse of over 10,000 banks and non-bank institutions, including shadow banks like trusts, amid a credit crunch and speculative bubble (which the Fed may have contributed to). The Fed's response to this crisis has been criticized by economists like Milton Friedman for its failure to lower interest rates or provide assistance to struggling banks. This event significantly impacted the role of the Fed.

Recall from our earlier discussions, in the current fractional reserve banking system, most money in the system (~94%) is actually credit. So, when companies/banks/individuals default, the loans are written down, and money is actually destroyed- it is deleted from the ledgers of banks. This is the nasty dual sword of credit- it creates money in good times, leading to increased revenues, asset values increasing, business growth, employment, etc. However, every dollar lent out has to be repaid. These dollars need to be paid back as the economy starts to roll over, and when they aren't, the money they constituted is eliminated from the system. M3 Money Supply fell an estimated 30% during the Great Depression. (The Fed mysteriously stopped tracking M3 Money Supply in the early days of the Great Financial Crisis).

Thus, the widespread collapse in prices that began in 1929 on Black Monday was not just due to overleveraged speculators on the stock market- if that were the case, it would have just been an equity bear market and perhaps a mild recession (like the 2000 Tech Bubble, where DotCom stocks fell 80%, but the general economy pulled back only slightly). The continued spiraling drops in prices of everything, from homes, to bread, to oil- was a result of the actual destruction of money that was occurring in the banking system. As credit was destroyed, money was as well- and with fewer dollars chasing the same goods, the dollars became more valuable, and thus it required fewer of them to purchase real goods. Add onto that the hoarding of cash, which reduced money velocity, and prices fell even further. Businesses that were overleveraged were the first to default, but as prices continued to fall and revenues collapsed, even good businesses with sturdy credit could not find willing lenders. No one was willing to lend for fear of default. In response, the Fed's powers were expanded substantially. It had seen small trials of the Open Market Operations in 1907 and again in 1923, and in 1933 used this procedure again, although it did not use it to its full effect as it would in 2008. Open market operations (OMO) refer to the practice of buying and selling U.S. Treasury securities, along with other securities, on the open market in order to regulate the supply of money that is on reserve in U.S. banks. This supply is what's available to loan out to businesses and consumers. The Fed purchases Treasury securities to increase the supply of money and sells them to reduce the supply of money.

The Fed can thus influence the Price (interest rates) and Quantity (M2 Money Supply) of Money itself- and by doing so, indirectly affect the prices of everything else in an economy. Again, this practice was originally limited to only U.S. Treasuries, but it would be expanded in future crises to include mortgage backed securities (2008), and corporate bond ETFs (2020). During the latter part of the 1930's, as part of their bid to widen the powers of the Fed, Federal Reserve Governors adopted the "mandate" of ensuring full employment (or as close to it as they can muster), in a bid to shift the overall strategy from solely bank lending to a more holistic monetary policy view. During the inflationary 1970's, Congress added new stipulations to the Federal Reserve Act of 1913, so that now the Fed aims to follow their dual mandate of price stability and full employment. In the aftermath of the Great Depression, many monetary scholars envisioned a re-imagined Federal Reserve. The Fed, they argued, should work to eliminate the business cycles all together. However, economic cycles are part and parcel of civilizational development and have existed for millennia-the Kondratieff Cycle, for example, is an 80 year economic super cycle borne out of technological innovation. Credit cycles have been observed for hundreds of years, and consistently caused spurs in economic growth followed by subsequent recession.

The business cycle is an upwards trending sine wave, where credit creation fuels economic expansion for a time, and then the economy begins to roll over, and all these debts become due, and thus a recession/depression occurs. The cycle has been seen in countries as different as Japan, Afghanistan, the U.S., China, and Brazil- and has even been observed in biblical times (debt Jubilees, Leviticus 25) as well as ancient Egypt, Rome, and Mesopotamia.

Financial Gravity And The Event Horizon

Economics is a social science- it is a blend of both humanities (sociology, psychology) and hard sciences (science, math, statistics). That being said, there are fundamental laws that govern economic systems wherever they prop up. In my personal life, my father has a PhD in Atmospheric Science- he was fascinated by how ice crystals and condensation are formed in clouds, and traveled the world (Chile, Antarctica, Canada) studying cloud physics. As a boy and basically an only child, he instilled a love of science in me- and I still view many things through that prism. When I explain economic concepts to him,

I like to use physics metaphors to get the point across, because this is the world he understands. To me, debt is a form of financial mass.

One of the emergent properties of mass is gravity, as described by Newton's equation. The mathematical formula for gravitational force is:

F= G((m1*m2)/(r^2))

The more mass an object has, the greater its gravitational pull, (multiplied by the gravitational constant, G). The distance between two objects in space is represented by r. The gravitational force gets weaker by the square of the distance between two masses. Debt is very much the same. At first, when debt is added onto an economy, it stimulates growth, as it creates new credit for businesses to build factories, train workers, construct buildings, etc. But, as the debt continues to grow, so do the interest payments- at some point, the debt load is too heavy, and the mass of the credit on the economy causes it to fall into itself in a contraction- leading to defaults and deflation.

Let's say you own a company making net income of $100M a year. With a debt load of $1B and an interest rate of 7%, you have to pay $70M a year in interest alone just to keep the creditors off your back. If for some reason the company's income falls to $50M, or interest rates rise, say to 11%- then you can't pay your debt. The math doesn't add up. The reason why debt cycles exist is as fundamental as the laws of physics; when an entity can't pay its debts, or even cover the interest on the debt- what happens? It defaults. This isn't a machination of political pundits, or econ professors, or conspiracy theorists- it is simply a law of math. When this happens across an entire sector, that's when you get deflation, credit contraction, and a downturn in the business cycle. If an entity can't pay back their loans, they default- who would want to lend money to an entity that can never pay them back, such as Evergrande? No one.

This is why I compare some economic laws (such as debt) to those of physics- both systems are ruled by math, the fundamental law of the universe. Finance at its heart is about numbers, and the math doesn't lie. When the numbers don't add up, and you have more liabilities than you can ever pay back, you default. "But wait!" you say, "governments issue debt in their own currency, which they print. Thus they can never default! Problem solved!" Potato, potahto. If they print money to stave off the default, they only devalue their currency- thus, they don't default in nominal terms (they DO pay back your $1,000 Treasury Bond) but in real terms (that $1,000 buys less stuff due to inflation).

Post Great Depression, the Fed began to take responsibility for trying to control the business cycle, as they had just seen how destructive a credit bust could be. Thus, the Fed decided to take on a role of "regulating" the cycle. It would do this by lowering interest rates and easing monetary conditions during a recession, spurring borrowing and lessening the rates of default, to make sure companies can continue to hire and train workers as needed. During economic booms, they would tighten monetary policy, to prevent the economy from "overheating" by increasing interest rates, thereby tightening monetary conditions and preventing excessive speculation and overleveraging. They also do this to get interest rates high enough so that they can drop them once again during a crisis, as interest rate policy is one of their most critical tools. An overheating economy sees excessive credit growth, which often creates inflation- this is why inflation tends to peak before a recession. Just as many have pointed out in this sub, the last time inflation was above 5% was right before the Great Financial Crisis of '08. Look at their own tracking of the Federal Funds Rate, the interest rate at which depository institutions trade federal funds (balances held at Federal Reserve Banks) with each other overnight, with the shaded areas indicating recessions.[46]

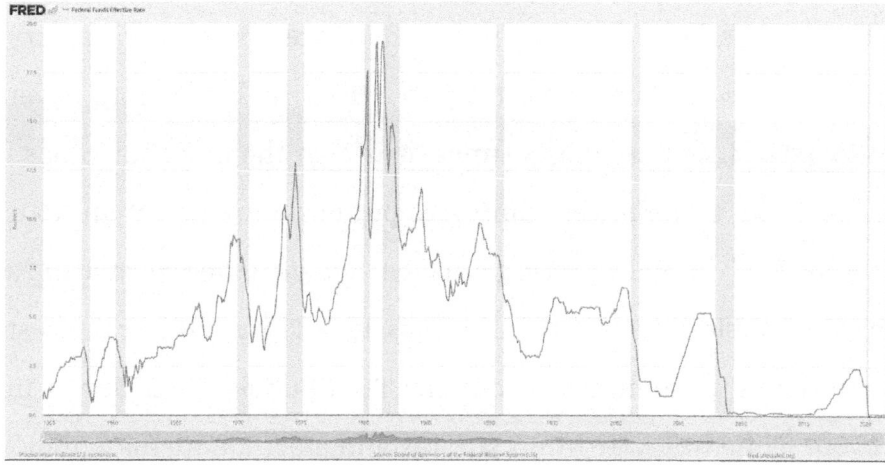

After every recession begins, they drop interest rates down to mitigate the hit of the downturn. As the economy improves, they are able to raise them back up again. It's a near perfect lagging indicator of a recession. How long do they keep interest rates down once they are in a recession? No one really knows. The Fed is perpetually caught in a catch-22; if they raise interest rates too soon during a recession, they worsen it or cause a depression. But, if they keep interest rates low to spur an upturn in the credit cycle (bubble in this case), then they are sowing the seeds for the next crash, as the debt created on the way up must be paid back on the way back down. When the economy is booming, if they raise interest rates too fast), then they cause debt payments to spike, which means defaults occur, and the economy starts to roll over.

There is no real escape from this conundrum. As you can see, the Fed has been fighting it for the better part of a century to no avail- it keeps reacting to crises in hindsight, never understanding that many times, it is also the one that caused it- Just like a firefighter coming to put out a fire he set an hour before. Each bubble bursting must be met with the Fed creating a bigger bubble. 1990 sees a mild recession? Time to lower interest rates and ("accidentally") spur the Tech Bubble. That bursts in 2000? Time to lower interest rates and start a housing bubble. That collapses? Start an Everything Bubble in 2009. Rinse and repeat.

This process continually creates more debt, more inflated assets, and more risk in the system. Look at the chart above- you'll notice that the troughs (low interest) get larger and deeper, and the peaks get shorter- with each crisis, they are able to raise the rate to a lower level than before, and have to drop it to a deeper level than before, to get themselves out of it.

Pre 1990, the Fed Funds rate was at 9.5%. In 2000 it hit a cycle high of 6.5%. Pre 2008 it barely got above 5%, then it was pinned to near zero after the housing crisis until Yellen finally decided to start hiking in late 2015, but even then it took three years to get to a measly 2.4%, and even that could be held for only a couple months. Why do they keep lowering interest rates, and keeping them lower than before? Simple, just look at a chart of public debt to GDP for the United States. As the Fed has continued with this game, debt as a percent of GDP has continually increased, from a starting point of 30% in 1981 to 132% where we sit today. Ever increasing levels of debt means the federal government will go bankrupt if interest rates stay at historic norms (6-8%), so the Fed has worked to suppress interest rates to keep the Treasury solvent.

The Fed, with this trend of lower and lower interest rates in their vain attempt to kill the credit cycle, have created a financial black hole- the more they lower rates to get out and stave off default, the more debt is created, piling on more and more mass. This pushes interest rates even lower, which creates more loan demand, and thus more debt, in a devastating feedback loop. This game will continue until the whole thing collapses under the weight of it's own gravity. That, or they burn their way out with inflation. There has been much discussion of a taper, that the Fed will stop printing money to buy securities and will raise interest rates to "fight inflation". To me, anyone who believes they will accomplish this is being foolish. The Fed could barely get interest rates above 2.4% in late 2018 before the stock market began to fall into bear market territory and the repo market blew up in September 2019. What makes them think they could get interest rates high enough to matter to fight inflation (above 7%) with debt to GDP 30% higher than it was in

2019?

Each time they begin this program, the markets react violently. Addicted to the heroin of easy money and low interest rates, the prisoners of this system, the banks and the U.S. Treasury itself, are up to their eyeballs in debt, and any attempt to offload that debt is vehemently opposed. Disconnecting the Fed's liquidity hose results in immediate withdrawal and must be put back quickly if the Fed wants to avoid a full blown deflationary spiral. The prisoners demand ever increasing liquidity, more and more QE, and tapers (pull backs in money printing) become ever shorter and fewer.

The inmates are running the asylum.

Bernanke assured everyone during the Financial Crisis that quantitative easing "would be temporary, and the tapers would be permanent". It appears the opposite is true- QE is permanent, and the tapers are temporary. They can only taper for a little while until something else blows up and they are forced to start printing again. Much like a black hole, in many ways we cannot directly observe the phenomenon, but we can see its effects on what surrounds it. The financial gravity the Fed has created by incentivizing ever more borrowing has caused more and more distortions in financial markets, pumping some sectors to absurdly high levels and creating shortages in others.

The weight of the debt is pulling the economy and markets down, but with constant money printing the Fed hopes to stave off disaster. Much like a black hole however, the process is exponential, and the longer the Fed keeps interest rates at the zero bound, the harder it will be to escape and the more money they'll have to print to get out. For those of us who follow economics/monetary policy, this exact scenario played out in the fall of 2018- the Fed stopped QE, and reducing its balance sheet. The markets, a month later, started nosediving. I was actually on Wall Street at the time coincidentally doing interviews, and touring the banks for job offers- however I never ended up working there.

I talked to a lot of analysts, they all said that this turbulence was bad, with no more Fed support the markets were due for a correction. But they also confidently asserted that the Fed would change its mind and start QE again once things got bad enough. The taper, they said, would not last forever. The markets would make the Fed blink. Sure enough, they were right. From August to mid-December, major equity indexes dropped 20%, putting them in a technical bear market. I was there in late October, and pretty much every day saw heavy selling. December got even worse, and as the selling continued, worry began to spread across financial markets. Powell stuck to his guns and insisted the balance sheet reduction would continue barring another financial crisis. Here's a quote from an article on December 19th, 2018:[47]

"Minutes into his press conference on December 19, Powell was asked if the Fed is looking into altering its strategy of undoing quantitative easing by allowing its massive holdings of Treasuries and mortgage-backed securities to mature off the balance sheet. "I think that the runoff (reduction) of the balance sheet has been smooth and has served its purpose and I don't see us changing that," Powell said, adding that interest rates would continue to be the "active tool of monetary policy." When Janet Yellen kicked off the unwind process at the end of 2017, the Fed outlined its intention to let the roll-off occur on "auto-pilot" with no promise of reverting back to quantitative easing — unless there were a "sufficient" negative shock to the economy."

Dec 24th, 2018, saw a big drop in the markets, a 400 point loss in the Dow, marking the third Friday in a row of red days in the indices. Again, this entire bear market occurred without an external economic shock or a default by a major American bank- it was purely driven by the fear that the Fed would not restart QE and the taper would continue.

Not even two weeks later, everything changed. The Fed Chairman, Jerome Powell, came out and recanted his earlier statement of a tapering program "on autopilot". He said they'd stop tapering soon and may even begin QE again after they'd "re-examined the situation". Markets rebounded, and after QE began again in the fall of that year, they started rallying hard.[48]

Many market observers did not understand the implications of what just happened. What many others grasped, and what I was beginning to suspect, was that this series of events was a major signpost that something was seriously wrong in equity markets. **The markets were completely dependent on Fed liquidity, and the Fed had blown a bubble in literally every single asset class in the financial markets- this bubble was able to be maintained only through constant (and growing) QE, and any taper of these injections resulted in immediate collapse of the bubble.**

December 2018 demonstrated that the removal of that liquidity heroin that the markets were addicted to resulted in rapid downward re-pricing of financial assets. The "wealth effect" the Fed had created was nothing more than an illusion. Something had changed since 2008. Although the NBER (National Bureau of Economic Research) claimed that we had only experienced a recession, if we use their original terminology we actually had been through a depression. Depressions were originally defined as prolonged periods of economic underperformance, which by all indications we were experiencing. GDP nominally was rising, but much of that could be attributed to increased government spending (component of GDP) and inflation (raw GDP is not adjusted for inflation).

NBER estimates we underperformed GDP potential by around $8.2 trillion in real growth since '08, which would have mostly gone to middle and working class workers in the form of wages.[49] Although there were no more bank failures after the fall of '08, unemployment spread throughout the economy, growth slowed to a standstill, and many left the workforce altogether. If we divide the performance of the S&P 500 by the Fed's balance sheet since the financial crisis, the line is flat! This means that there has been basically NO REAL growth in stock prices since 2008- with the only rise in prices due to money printing.

The correlation coefficient between central bank quantitative easing and the price of stock indexes is nearly 1. The money printed by the Fed, because of the structure of the open market operations, is plugged directly into the Treasury markets, and from there, flows into equities and derivatives. This has served to primarily enrich the asset owners, financial institutions, and wealthy elites who own the majority of the stock market anyways.

The entire rally has been an illusion, financed by the Fed and maintained through QE. In the black expanse of space, many things are not what they seem.

Each crisis requires exponentially more stimulus to be used to fight it- $100 billion for the tech bubble. $2.2 trillion for 2008. $4.1 trillion (and climbing) for March 2020. The Fed is running out of time. They will almost undoubtedly try to taper to escape. Even if they try this, it will fail in time, causing a rapid collapse in asset prices. When it does, they will have to turn back the liquidity hose even more than before, as they try to escape the event horizon, "the point of no return" where not even light itself can run fast enough to flee the massive gravitational pull of the black hole.

What they do not grasp yet is that they have already crossed the event horizon. Only hard choices lie ahead - the only thing on their mind will be avoiding another Great Depression, but to do this they will have to print trillions more. This will only accelerate worsening inflation and unleash devastating feedback loops that lurk under the surface of our economy. Many a State has wrecked itself on these shores, but sadly few heed the warnings. As stated in an Artemis Capital paper,

"On cold nights when the moon is full you can watch these

ghost ships (economies) making their journey back to hell... they appear to warn us that our resolution to avoid one fate, may damn us to the other."[50]

THE SWORD OF DAMOCLES

Economic Warfare & The End of Bretton Woods"

T he story of the "Sword of Damocles," can be traced back to the ancient Roman philosopher Cicero. Cicero included the tale in his book "Tusculan Disputations," which was published in 45 B.C. In Cicero's version of the story, the tyrannical king Dionysius II, who ruled over the city of Syracuse in the 4th and 5th centuries B.C., serves as the central character. The tale is meant to illustrate the dangers of greed and power and has been widely referenced throughout history as a cautionary tale. Despite being wealthy and influential, Dionysius was deeply unhappy. He had many enemies due to his oppressive rule and was constantly worried about being assassinated. As a result, he took extreme measures to protect himself, sleeping in a room surrounded by a moat and only allowing his daughters to shave his beard with a razor. Despite his precautions, Dionysius was unable to escape his fears and remained unhappy.

Dionysius became particularly upset one day when a court flatterer named Damocles showered him with compliments and remarked on how wonderful Dionysius's life must be. Dionysius, annoyed by these comments, asked Damocles if he would like to experience this supposedly wonderful life for himself. When Damocles eagerly agreed, Dionysius allowed him to sit on a golden couch and ordered a group of servants to wait on him and provide him with delicious food and fragrant perfumes and ointments. However, despite these luxurious trappings, Dionysius's dissatisfaction remained. Damocles was thrilled to be treated like a king, but as he began to enjoy this luxurious lifestyle, he noticed that Dionysius had also placed a sharp sword over his head, hanging from the ceiling by a single strand of horsehair.

After noticing the sword hanging above him, Damocles became consumed with fear for his life and was no longer able to fully enjoy the lavish feast or the attentions of the servants. Despite initially being excited about his temporary royal treatment, Damocles eventually asked to be excused, stating that he no longer wanted to be so fortunate. Damocles' story is a cautionary tale of being careful of what you wish for- Those who strive for power often unknowingly create the very systems that lead to their own eventual downfall. The Sword is often used as a metaphor for a looming danger; a hidden trap that can obliterate those unaware of the great risk that hegemony brings.

Heavy lies the head which wears the crown.

The Dollar as a WMD

Most Americans today walk around aware of the fact that they are a superpower. Military parades, fighter jet flyovers at football games, and clips showing American soldiers engaging enemy combatants are commonplace. However, what most Americans do not know, is the secret mighty Excalibur that the U.S. government wields in order to achieve most of its ends- the dollar itself.

Since the end of WWII, many conflicts have been resolved through sanctions and negotiation, at the direction of the United States. In almost every case, the U.S. has used the Treasury and its control over the banking system, to effectively choke and strangle powerful opponents without ever firing a single shot.

This system is best described by Joseph Wang, a former senior trader at the Federal Reserve's open market desk, in his book Central Banking 101:[51]

"The Eurodollar system is offshore, but ultimately, all dollar banking transactions no matter the origin will have a link to the U.S. banking system. After all, offshore dollars would not really be dollars if they were not fungible with onshore dollars. The U.S. government has authority over the U.S. banking system, and by extension, over the offshore banking system. **This implies that the US government has authority over virtually every dollar transaction done through the banking system in the entire world.** Let's walk through an example to see how this works. Suppose a bank in Kazakhstan named Kbank has a dollar loan business. Kbank makes a $1000 loan to its client and credits its clients account for $1000. The client then withdraws that $1000 to pay a supplier who banks with a US Bank (named Ubank). Kbank is going to have to settle a payment of $1000 with Ubank.

There are two ways it can do this:

If it has a reserve account at the Fed, then it can send Ubank a wire for $1000 in reserves OR

If it holds its dollars as a bank deposit at a U.S. Commercial Bank, then it will have to ask that commercial bank to send Ubank $1000 in reserves.

In the second case, Kbank's commercial bank will send $1000 in reserves to Ubank while reducing Kbank's deposit balance on its books by $1000. In either example, the transaction must go through the U.S. banking system. **The U.S. government, through its control of the U.S. banking system, has the power to shut anyone out of the dollar banking system.** If the U.S. government decides that someone should be sanctioned, then that person will not be able to receive or send dollars through banks anywhere in the world."

SWIFT is not so much a payments mechanism as it is a communication network; but without access to it payments cannot be verified and many counterparty banks may not transact with you. For this reason, being cut out of the SWIFT network is a grave risk for banks and could essentially destroy their ability to transfer funds on behalf of customers.

See below for some more examples of newspaper headlines- and ALL of these are banks located outside the US:

- The Guardian 11/4/2015 - Deutsche Bank fined $258m for violating US sanctions
- New York Times 10/15/2019- U.S. Indicts Turkish Bank on Charges of Evading Iran Sanctions
- Reuters 4/9/2019- Standard Chartered to pay $1.1 billion for sanctions violations
- Mercury News 4/3/2018- Report: Bahrain bank helped Iran evade sanctions for years

The list goes on and on. Again, these are all foreign banks-the United States technically has no jurisdiction here! This was elaborated on in a book called "Treasury's War" by Juan Zarate, a former senior Treasury official and architect of modern financial warfare.

This may not seem a big deal on the surface- these countries are enemies of the United States, right? But this demonstrates how U.S. policy can overrule the policy of sovereign nations such as France. France had no such sanctions against these countries-but the U.S. Treasury Department can effectively force French banks to follow American guidelines!

Imagine if China had this power- and demanded that Canada could not trade with Taiwan, cutting both countries off from the international monetary system if they did so. To many foreign officials, America has become drunk with this power, and is using it to tyrannize other countries to follow our foreign policy. (Again, I am not arguing in defense of countries like Iran, which have anti-democratic values, just demonstrating that the U.S. has immense power over even Western countries and can effectively set their foreign policy for them)

By sanctioning countries and cutting them out of the U.S. banking system, the Treasury can effectively send them back to the Stone Age. Iran, for example, now has extreme difficulty in settling currency for oil and gas contracts- and has even defaulted to pricing its oil in gold in order to receive payment![52]

Many other countries are chafing under this dollar dominant system. See below for an excerpt of recent headlines taken from Mr. X Interviews Volume II:[53]

- 5/22/18- Bloomberg- US Sanction power may be reaching its limit, "response to Iran shows global economy won't be bossed around forever"
  - "You f***ing Americans", the message read. "Who are you to tell us, the rest of the world, that we're not going to deal with Iranians?" - UK banker, 2012
- 5/28/18- Reuters- India says it only follows UN sanctions, not unilateral US sanctions on Iran
- 5/9/18- Associated Press- Australia and Japan still support Iran Deal
- 6/6/18- Bloomberg- Merkel warns of G-7 split over Trump's "America First", says World becoming "re-ordered globally"

The United States, by controlling the world reserve currency, wields immense economic and financial power over most of the globe. However, this power corrupts and corrodes the host over time- and warning signs are beginning to appear signaling that America's time as global economic hegemon may be coming to an end.

The Unraveling of the Global Monetary System

Before we continue, let us do a quick review of the essential paradox of reserve currencies- Triffin's Dilemma. In August 1971, after the closing of the gold window, the dollar was officially off the gold standard. In the turmoil that followed, currency markets began to experience rapid volatility and signs of inflation began to appear. Many G10 countries began to worry about the dollar's sustainability as a world reserve currency.

In a meeting of the G10 in late 1971 in Rome, U.S. Treasury Secretary Connally famously quipped,[54]

"The Dollar is OUR Currency, but YOUR problem!".

He was referring to Triffin's Dilemma, and the unfavorable effects it would have on developing countries while boosting American economic and thus political dominance. The dilemma refers to the tension that arises when a country's economic goals for the short term within its borders clash with its long-term objectives on the international stage, especially when its currency serves as a global reserve currency.

To recap:

- Post WWII, the U.S. dollar became the world reserve currency, and thus was used as a "reserve asset" by other central banks and as a settlement currency for international trade. This creates massive artificial demand for U.S. dollars and Treasuries, since these nations need them for trade and to hold in reserve in case of a crisis in their homeland (Thailand in 1997)

- This global demand for dollars means America has to be a net exporter of dollars. The opposite side of the trade of dollars is goods/investments, and thus the U.S. has to be a net importer, or in other words, run trade deficits.

- This means the U.S. has to consume more than it produces, and give out more investment than it makes domestically. In other words, they have to run a negative current account, pushing more dollars to the world on net.

- Over time, this leads to a surplus of debt and consumption, and a lack of investment and production.

- For example, manufacturing jobs thus get transferred overseas, bolstering the economy of foreign countries (China) and weakening the host country (U.S.). This loss of manufacturing means wage deflation/stagnation in the

U.S. as domestic jobs disappear

- Thus, contributing to political polarization and economic despair, rising rates of depression/suicide and drug abuse, homelessness

- The artificial demand for Treasuries also lowers borrowing costs massively, inducing the U.S. government to borrow and spend more than it otherwise would, creating fiscal deficits and unsustainable levels of debt.

- Eventually, the United States will reach a breaking point, where the manufacturing base is completely gone, and the debt levels are so high, that foreign creditors will not lend it money anymore.

- When this happens, the government's only recourse is to either slash spending immediately (which will lead to severe recession) or print dollars, which will lead to rampant inflation.

- The endgame is the replacement of the world reserve currency with a new one, which can cause horrible inflation, as the old reserve currency loses demand and all overseas dollars come back to the U.S. to roost.

(Below is a graphic of the results of the U.S. being a reserve currency holder from the point of view of a developing country, Liberia)

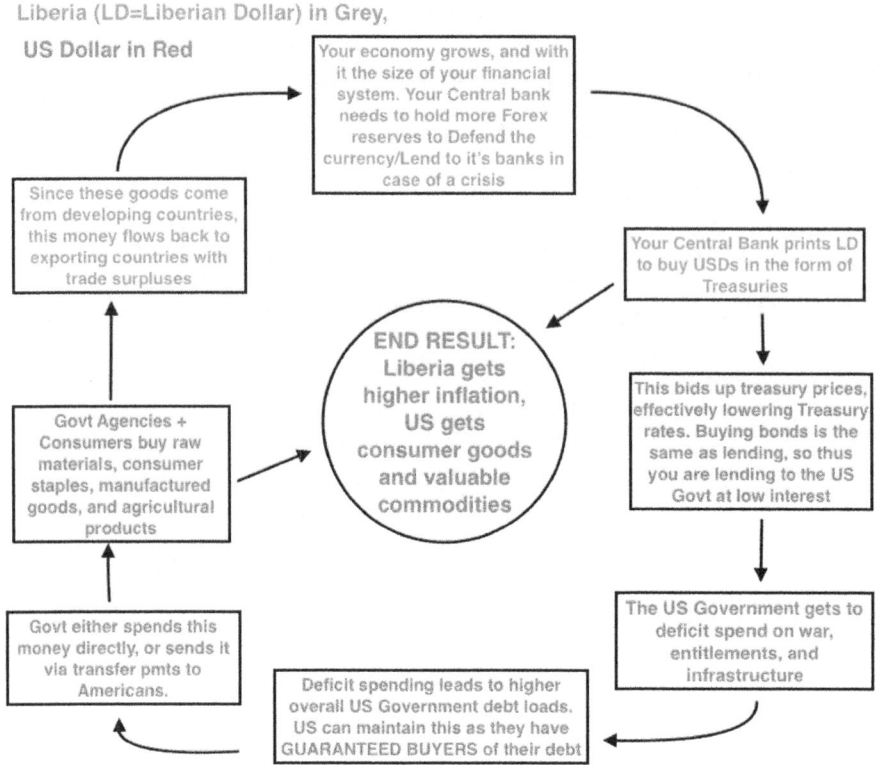

The trade deficit was mostly propped up in the 1950s and 1960s as Europe rebuilt after the carnage of WW2 and the US was able to be a manufacturing powerhouse, producing goods domestically and exporting them to other nations. Global trade was limited, and America was the center of the world economy. After 1974, and the entry of the Petrodollar system, and balance of trade deteriorated significantly as global trade boomed and the U.S. began to constantly export dollars as other nations industrialized and began producing goods to be sold in the developed world.

Lyn Alden summarizes the issue perfectly:[55]

"When most other countries run trade deficits, they eventually have a big enough currency devaluation so that their exports become more competitive and importing becomes more expensive, which usually prevents multi-decade extremes from building up. However, because the petrodollar system creates persistent international demand for the dollar, it means the US trade deficit never is allowed to correct and balance itself out. The trade deficit is held open persistently by the structure of the global monetary system, which creates a permanent imbalance, and is the flaw that eventually, after a long enough timeline, brings the system down."

For those of us who follow monetary economics closely, omens of the death of the dollar as world reserve currency are beginning to appear. We'll start with Treasuries, the backbone of the global financial system.

Remember, foreigners must recycle their trade surpluses back in USDs in order to settle global trade and hold enough currency reserves in their central banks. Historically, they did so by buying Treasuries, since these are considered "risk free assets". See Foreign Holdings of Federal Debt, below.[56]

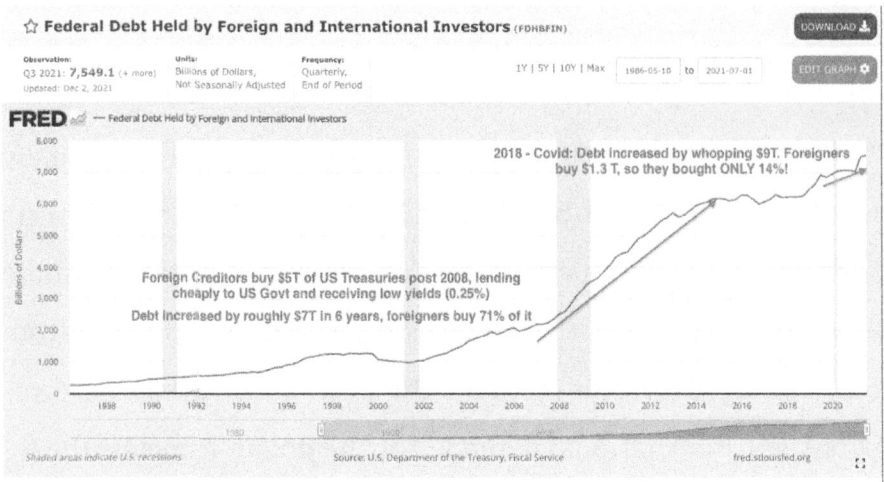

☆ **Federal Debt Held by Foreign and International Investors** (FDHBFIN)

Observation:	Units:	Frequency:
Q3 2021: **7,549.1** (+ more)	Billions of Dollars,	Quarterly,
Updated: Dec 2, 2021	Not Seasonally Adjusted	End of Period

1Y | 5Y | 10Y | Max   1986-05-10 to 2021-07-01   EDIT GRAPH ⚙   DOWNLOAD ⬇

FRED — Federal Debt Held by Foreign and International Investors

2018 - Covid: Debt increased by whopping $9T. Foreigners buy $1.3 T, so they bought ONLY 14%!

Foreign Creditors buy $5T of US Treasuries post 2008, lending cheaply to US Govt and receiving low yields (0.25%)

Debt increased by roughly $7T in 6 years, foreigners buy 71% of it

Shaded areas indicate U.S. recessions   Source: U.S. Department of the Treasury, Fiscal Service   fred.stlouisfed.org

After the 2008 financial crisis, the U.S. government began borrowing heavily to pay for programs like TARP and increased unemployment benefits. The majority of this borrowing was backstopped by foreign creditors, who bought around 70% of the new debt issued (the Fed bought most of the rest). But, since 2014-2015, foreign central banks began easing up on their purchases of Treasuries. So much so, in fact, that their holdings began to flatline, and there were no (or very low) net increases for several years. This is surprising given the fact that the trade deficits were still increasing, so the U.S. was still sending out more dollars into the world than it received!

From 2018 to now, federal debt ballooned by a whopping $9T ($21T back then to $30T today), but foreigners only bought a measly 14% (1.3T) of it. Again, a drastic decrease from their buying patterns of prior years. So, this begs the question; where are their surplus dollars ending up? They still need to recycle their dollar surpluses effectively- one easy way to do this is to buy assets denominated in USD (equities, real estate, etc.). So, they have started massively investing in American assets, as reflected by the Net International Investment Position (NIIP), shown below:[57]

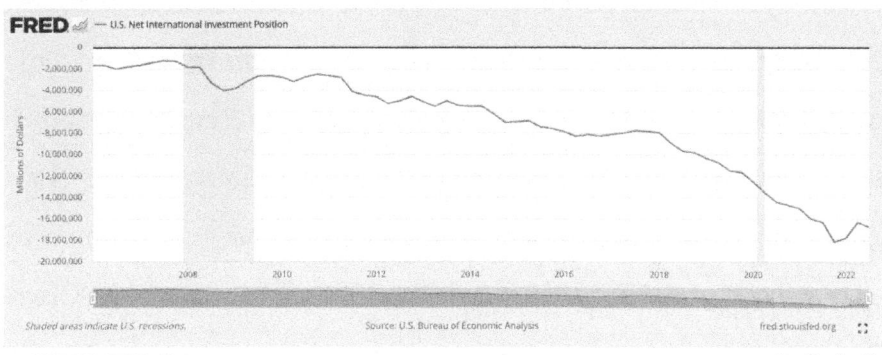

(The Net International Investment Position of a country measures how much foreign assets they own, minus how much of their assets that foreigners own, and the chart above shows it as a percentage of GDP. As of 2021, the United States owns $29 trillion in foreign assets, while foreigners own $42 trillion in US assets, including US government bonds, corporate bonds, stocks, and real estate.)

This represents a negative 60% NIIP, and has fueled the creation of a massive stock and real estate bubble. All this massive investment has helped to boost economic growth in the past- however it also creates systemic risk. With foreigners owning so much American assets, it means that a large proportion of wealth creation is being siphoned overseas, and doesn't recycle back into American communities. This contributes to wealth inequality globally, and in the U.S. as well. Further, this creates the potential for a massive "rug-pull" on the American economy. If foreign investors began to lose confidence in the U.S. economy, they could essentially begin a run on the dollar. This would begin by massive sales of Treasuries, but could spread to stocks and real estate, causing widespread deflation worse than 2008. The Fed would then be faced with the grim choice of either letting $42T of US assets be fire-sold into a New Great Depression, or ramp up quantitative easing to buy the assets on sale- untold trillions of dollars would need to be printed. This would make the current QE program look like a joke in comparison.

(Again, this is a worse-case scenario; I am not asserting that it will happen, but an event like this could be one of the triggers for much worse inflation, and indeed, potential extreme inflation.)

Many of these countries do not necessarily want to invest in U.S. assets, especially Treasuries- but they are forced to due to the structure of the system and the fact that there just isn't any good alternative (for now). For countries that are geo-political rivals of the U.S., this system is an extremely potent force to help the U.S. maintain status as an economic superpower. This was put best by Charles Duelfer, quoted in the book Mr. X Interviews Volume II:[58]

"Look at the world (or even just the United States) from the position of China. What makes America a superpower? Is it the military? Partly. Is it nuclear weapons? Not so much. What really gives us leverage is the position of the dollar as the base currency. In the last financial crisis, we escaped largely by printing money. Other countries can't get away with that without causing massive inflation. Sitting in Beijing, it could be seen as a financial attack -- US Treasury printing tons of dollars that has the effect of exporting inflation to other countries. We borrow money (by selling treasuries to finance our wars, debt, TARP, etc.) and then pay them off by, in essence, printing dollars. The role of the dollar as base currency is a uniquely powerful lever. It is one that is rarely thought of in terms of national security, but nothing is more important. If we lose it, we will have lost our position as the last super power. Period."

These rivals, particularly Russia, China and Iran, have been hurt the worst by US sanctions and economic warfare. They are also at the forefront in trying to displace the dollar as reserve currency in order to strip the United States of its "exorbitant privilege

See the below headlines for reference, from Luke Gromen:[59]

- 8/14/14- Reuters- Putin says USD monopoly in global energy trade is damaging economy

- 11/26/10- Telegraph- Putin: It's quite possible Russia could join EU currency zone, create currency that would eclipse the USD

- 6/1/15- Financial Times- Russian Oil Giant Gazprom begins selling oil to China in renminbi (CNY) rather than dollars

- 6/24/15- Reuters- China likely to get nod for CNY gold fix soon, could compel foreign suppliers to pay in CNY

- 9/14/17- Nikkei Asia- China aims for dollar-free oil trade

- 10/11/17- CNBC- Saxo Bank: USD reserve status at risk as China begins to de-dollarize

- 10/14/17- Barrons- The petrodollar system is being undermined- Barrons

- 11/20/13- Bloomberg- PBOC (Central Bank of China) says no longer in China's interest to boost FX reserves (aka buy USDs)

- 9/12/17- Bloomberg- US Treasury Sec Mnuchin threatens banning China from "dollar system" (SWIFT)

- 8/24/17- Reuters- Saudis may seek funding in CNY (Chinese Yuan)

- 2/16/16- The Epoch Times- Chinese general says contain the US by attacking its finances

These countries aren't alone- as we have already covered, even allies such as the United Kingdom, India, Germany, and others are tired of being exploited by this system. The exorbitant privilege created by Triffin's Dilemma means that these countries have to work hard to produce goods, which are swapped for dollars (which we can print out of thin air). They then have to exchange these dollars for U.S. assets instead of investing in their own countries. We get cheap goods and cheap debt, fueling our overly consumerist culture- while they get more inflation and less investment in their own economies. The ill-effects of Triffin's Dilemma are building up over time and corroding the very system which provides the U.S. with so much economic dominance.

In 2014/2015, on a net basis, global central banks stopped buying Treasuries. Essentially, they decided to stop funding growing U.S. deficits, which means that now the U.S. is on the hook for any new spending our government incurs. Credit to FFTT, LLC for the chart below:[60]

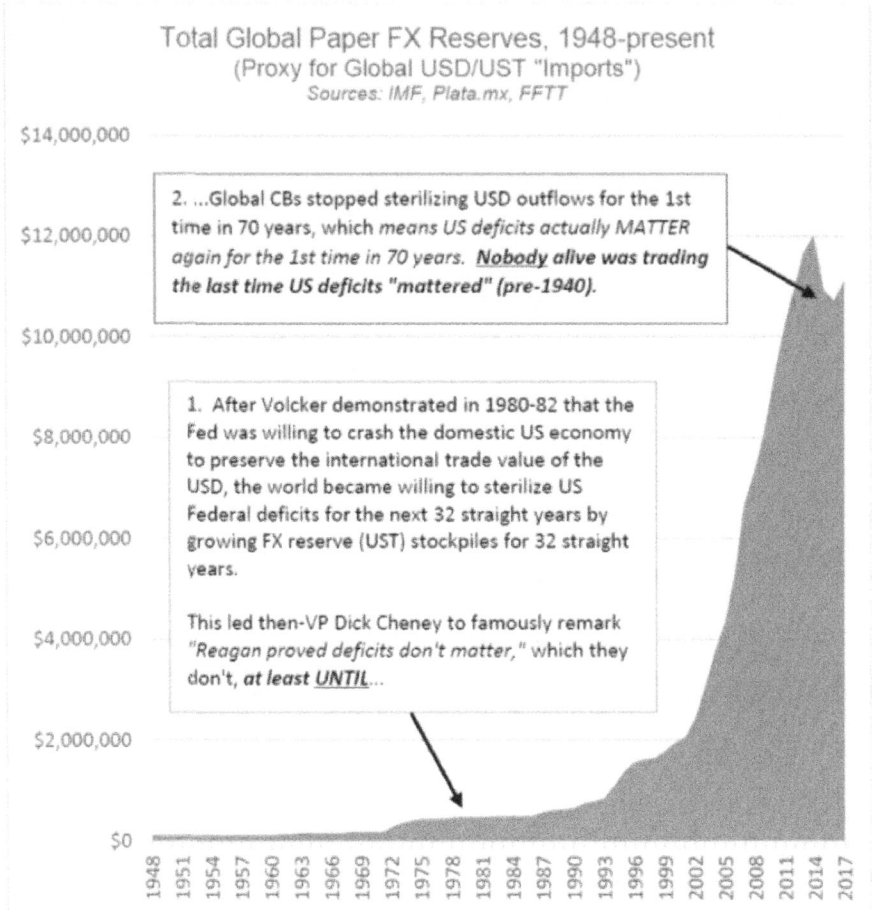

Total Global Paper FX Reserves, 1948-present
(Proxy for Global USD/UST "Imports")
Sources: IMF, Plata.mx, FFTT

2. ...Global CBs stopped sterilizing USD outflows for the 1st time in 70 years, which means *US deficits actually MATTER again for the 1st time in 70 years.* **Nobody alive was trading the last time US deficits "mattered" (pre-1940).**

1. After Volcker demonstrated in 1980-82 that the Fed was willing to crash the domestic US economy to preserve the international trade value of the USD, the world became willing to sterilize US Federal deficits for the next 32 straight years by growing FX reserve (UST) stockpiles for 32 straight years.

This led then-VP Dick Cheney to famously remark *"Reagan proved deficits don't matter,"* which they don't, *at least UNDERLINE...*

Since there is no (or very little) new lending coming into the United States from global central banks, we had to source it ourselves. This began with structural changes to Money Market

Funds and bank capital requirements (Basel III, Dodd-Frank) that forces MMFs and banks to buy Treasuries for their balance sheets. The amount of funds managed by government MMFs doubled from $0.8T in 2014 to $2.1T in 2016 and then $3.9T by 2020. These MMFs almost exclusively bought short maturity Treasuries (called T-bills), essentially becoming a new large lender for the US government.[61]

However, there was only so much money in the money markets for this, so it would only buy a limited amount of time. Beginning in March 2020, the federal government began massive fiscal expenditures to prop up the economy and deal with the fallout from Covid-19. This time was different - since global central banks were no longer lending wholesale to the U.S., we had to print the difference. The Fed had to step in and backstop the Treasury. American fiscal deficits, which "hadn't mattered" for 40 years, now began to matter!

Foreign central banks barely increased their Treasury holdings, and to ensure the government wouldn't go bankrupt, the Fed had to print trillions of dollars to buy up all the new debt being issued. The Fed directly monetizing spending by purchasing T-bills is harmful to the system- it is undoubtedly inflationary for the United States. This differs from the earlier state of affairs, where other central banks were forced to print and inflate their own currencies to get their hands on dollars and then invest these dollars back into American capital markets.

Lyn Alden expands on this point;

"That's not exactly how the "global reserve" currency is supposed to work. It's like a restaurant chef eating her own cooking more than her customers do. This is what other non-global-reserve countries look like. Within one year, the Fed went from owning half as much Treasuries as foreign central banks combined, to more than them combined."[62]

In 2008, when the Fed did this, the money had stayed in the banking system due to the nature of QE. However, now in 2020 it was the U.S. government and indeed the entire economy that needed to be bailed out, so that is where the dollars had to flow. This led to a massive influx of dollars into the real economy, and thus the recipe for a large surge in inflation in the coming years. With fiscal deficits running at $2.8 trillion in 2021, and foreign central banks only financing 14% of it, that means there is $2.4 trillion of Treasuries that need to be bought- the Fed will likely have to buy a substantial portion of it. Thus, the Fed will likely have to print over $1 trillion every year for the foreseeable future. Inflationary feedback loops, discussed earlier, will kick in, and these figures will grow. The Fed will have to print more and more just to keep the government afloat.

All the borrowing of the past is coming back to bite. In October 2022 federal government debt hit $31 Trillion! At $31 trillion, a 1% increase in interest rates means an additional $310B in interest payments annually that must be paid. Who will lend the Treasury this money as the government continues to borrow its way to insolvency, and inflation rates rise above 7%?

Answer: the lender of last resort- the Fed

It is no surprise therefore that cognizant leaders in foreign countries see the writing on the wall and have begun to de-dollarize. Would you want your own country's currency being invested in a "reserve asset" that is losing 7.5% of its value (more like 15%) every year, and is projected to lose even more as the debt payments come due? A 2017 paper published by the Bank of International Settlements called "Triffin: dilemma or myth?" restates the core issue perfectly:[63]

"The most common version of Triffin shifts his thesis from the capital account to the current account. It posits that the reserve currency country must run, or at least does run, persistent current account deficits to provide the rest of the world with reserves denominated in its currency (Zhou (2009), Camdessus and Icard (2011), Paul Volcker in Feldstein (2013), Prasad 2013)). "In doing so, it becomes more indebted to foreigners until the risk-free asset ceases to be risk-free" (Financial Times Lexicon (no date)).

[...]

As applied to the United States, the current account version of Triffin runs as follows. The global accumulation of dollar reserves requires the United States to run a current account deficit. Since desired reserves rise with world nominal GDP, which is growing faster than US nominal GDP, the growth of dollar reserves will raise US external indebtedness unsustainably. <u>Either the United States will not run the current account deficits, leading to an insufficiency of global reserves. Or US indebtedness will rise without limit, undermining the value of the dollar and the reserves denominated in it.</u>"

The elites understand this issue perfectly- but the reason the system did so well for so long is that the U.S. debt levels were manageable, and there were structural advantages the US had that helped it immensely (deep and liquid bond + stock markets, large population, large % of global trade). But they also understand that Triffin's dilemma is the final nail in the coffin- it has meant that every country has lasted as a reserve currency holder for an average of only 80 years!

To put it another way, the host country (USA) has to decide to either not print dollars and import goods, which halts global trade (not enough $$ to settle trade) and causes defaults for third world countries with debt denominated in dollars,

OR

It has to decide to run current account deficits (to keep the global economy running) at the expense of burying itself in debt and de-industrializing the heartland, resulting in the US eventually having to print their way out (which will kill the USD as a world reserve currency holder).

The Fed, rushing to avoid a financial crisis in March 2020, printed trillions. This spurred inflation, which they then swore to fight. Thus, they began hiking interest rates on March 16th, and began quantitative tightening during the summer of 2022. QE had stopped- no new dollars were flowing out into a system which has a constant demand for them. Worse yet, they were hiking completely blind. Although the Fed is very far behind the curve, (meaning they are hiking far too late to really combat inflation)- other countries are even farther behind!

This is the basis for the Dollar Milkshake Theory put forth by Brent Johnson- the United States has built in global demand for its currency.[64] NO OTHER FIAT CURRENCY has this. This demand comes from central banks, who need dollars for foreign exchange reserves, import/export firms, who need dollars to settle trade invoices, third world governments, who borrow in dollars, and sovereign wealth funds, who need a secure and liquid place to invest their capital.

As the dollar rises, a vicious feedback loop emerges where countries must dump increasing amounts of their own currency in order to get their hands on USDs. This rise in DXY (the USD index) increases borrowing costs for countries and businesses with debts denominated in dollars, which puts severe strains on economic growth and forces more capital to flee into the U.S. to seek safe harbor.

Worse yet, the more the Fed raises rates, the more strain it exerts onto the system. Japan has rates currently at 0.00- 0.5%, and the Eurozone is at 1.25%. These central banks have barely begun hiking, and some even swear to keep them at the zero-bound. By hiking domestic interest rates above foreign ones, the Fed is incentivizing what are called carry trades. Since there is a spread between the Yen and the Dollar in terms of interest rates, it thus is profitable for traders to borrow in Yen (shorting it essentially) and buy Dollars, which can earn 2.25% interest. The spread would be around 2%.

DXY rises, and the Yen falls, in a vicious feedback loop. Thus, capital flows out of Japan, and into the United States. The U.S.

sucks up the dollar milkshake, draining global liquidity. As I've stated before, this has seriously dangerous implications for the global financial system; currently the Fed is not printing money, which is thus causing havoc in global trade (seen in the currency markets) because not enough dollars are flowing out to satisfy demand and financial conditions are tightening considerably.

The Fed must therefore restart QE and open dollar swap lines to other central banks unless it wants to spur a collapse on a global scale. All these foreign countries need to buy, borrow and trade in a currency that they cannot print! The largest factor in the strength of the DXY index by far is their desperate need for dollars. The Fed, knowingly or not, is basically in charge of the global financial system. They may shout, "We raise rates in the States to fight inflation, global consequences be damned!!". But that's a hell of a lot more difficult to follow when large G7 countries are in the early stages of a full-blown currency crisis.

The most serious implication of the Dollar Milkshake is that the Fed is responsible for supplying dollars to everyone. When they raise rates, they trigger a margin call on the entire world. They need to bail them out by supplying them with fresh dollars to stabilize their currencies.

In other words, the Fed must run the loosest and most

accommodative monetary policy worldwide- they must keep rates as low as possible, and print as much as possible, in order to keep the global financial system running. If they don't do that, sovereigns begin to blow up, like Japan did on September 22nd, 2022 and like England did a week later on September 28th.

And if the world's financial system implodes, they must bail out not only the United States, but virtually every global central bank. This is the Sword of Damocles. The money needed for this would be well in the dozens of trillions.

Most Americans today are unaware of the great benefits and might bestowed upon them due to the U.S. being the holder of a world reserve currency. Drunk with power, presidents from Nixon to Obama have started and continued large scale "forever wars" in Vietnam, Iraq, Afghanistan, and Yemen. Post Bretton Woods, the United States has become an empire, and essentially created financial colonies in most of the third world- by forcing them to use U.S. dollars, these countries subordinate their economies to support the value of the dollar, allowing America to borrow and spend recklessly without immediate consequence.

Further, by using USDs, these countries' banks are routed through the U.S. banking system and are thus subject to

American foreign policy, even policies that are not supported by the United Nations. The U.S. can essentially extend its jurisdiction over much of the global economy and cut off trade for those countries who protest. But this power comes with a cost- by exporting jobs, wages deflate across America and wealth inequality worsens. Political polarization quickly follows, along with the destabilization and corruption of institutions. The system requires ever increasing flows of dollars to satisfy demand, and the Fed will be forced to respond with a river of freshly printed greenbacks. Inflation that the U.S. has exported in the form of dollars is now a latent risk in the form of Treasuries held by foreigners.

A Sword of Damocles hangs precariously above our head. The drums of economic warfare have begun to beat. Can the United States survive the onslaught?

ENTER THE DRAGON

The Monster and the Simulacrum

"In the 1985 work "Simulacra and Simulation" French philosopher Jean Baudrillard recalls the Borges fable about the cartographers of a great Empire who drew a map of its territories so detailed it was as vast as the Empire itself. According to Baudrillard as the actual Empire collapses the inhabitants begin to live their lives within the abstraction believing the map to be real (his work inspired the classic film "The Matrix" and the book is prominently displayed in one scene).

The map is accepted as truth and people ignorantly live within a mechanism of their own design and the reality of the Empire is forgotten. This fable is a fitting allegory for our modern financial markets. Our fiscal well being is now prisoner to

financial and monetary engineering of our own design.

Central banking strategy does not hide this fact with the goal of creating the optional illusion of economic prosperity through artificially higher asset prices to stimulate the real economy.

While it may be natural to conclude that the real economy is slave to the shadow banking system this is not a correct interpretation of the Baudrillard philosophy-

The higher concept is that our economy IS the shadow banking system... the Empire is gone and we are living ignorantly within the abstraction. The Fed must support the shadow banking oligarchy because without it, the abstraction would fail."[65]

The Inflation Serpent

To most citizens living in the West, the concept of a collapsing fiat currency seems alien, unfathomable even. They regard it as an unfortunate event reserved only for those wretched souls unlucky enough to reside in third world countries or under brutal dictatorships. Monetary mismanagement was seen to be a symptom only of the most corrupt countries like Venezuela- those where the elites gained control of the Treasury and printing press and used this lever to steal unimaginable wealth while impoverishing their constituents.

However, the annals of history spin a different tale- in fact, an eventual collapse of fiat currency is the norm, not the exception. In a study of 775 fiat currencies created over the last 500 years, researchers found that approximately 599 have failed, leaving only 176 remaining in circulation. Approximately 20% of the 775 fiat currencies examined failed due to hyperinflation, 21%

were destroyed in war, and 24% percent were reformed through centralized monetary policy.[66] The remainder were either phased out, converted into another currency, or are still around today. The average lifespan for a pure fiat currency is only 27 years- significantly shorter than a human life.

Double-digit inflation, once deemed an "impossible" event for the United States, is now within a stone's throw. Powell, desperate to maintain credibility, has embarked on the most aggressive hiking schedule the Fed has ever undertaken. The cracks are starting to widen in the system. One has to look no further than a simple graph of the M2 Money Supply, a measure that most economists agree best estimates the total money supply of the United States, to see a worrying trend:

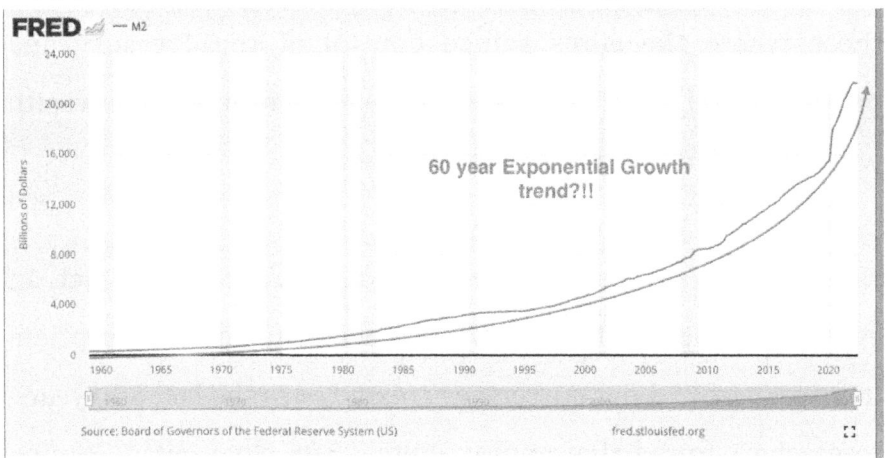

The trend is exponential. Through recessions, wars, presidential elections, cultural shifts, and even the deflationary Internet age- M2 keeps increasing non-linearly, with a positive second derivative- money supply growth is accelerating. This hyperbolic growth is indicative of a key underlying feature of the fiat money system: virtually all money is credit. Under a fractional reserve banking system, most money that circulates is loaned into existence, and doesn't exist as real cash- in fact, around 97% of all "money" counted within the banking system is debt, in one form or another. Debt virtually always has a yield- that yield is called interest, and that interest demands payment. Thus, any fiat money banking system MUST grow money supply at a compounding interest rate, forever, in order to remain stable. Debt defaulting is thus quite literally the destruction of money- which is why the deflation is widespread, and why M2 Money Supply shrank by 30% during the Great Depression.

Imagine that $0 exists in the money supply of a small town. You go to a local bank and post your house as collateral and ask to withdraw $100 as a loan, at 5% interest. The bank agrees, and deposits $100 into your account. They mark $100 as an asset (Loan Receivable) on their balance sheet, with the 5% earmarked as expected interest income. You go out and spend the money. It circulates in the town, at bars, restaurants, and hotels- the people are overjoyed to have a medium of exchange rather than using barter.

At the end of your loan term, the bank comes and asks for the $100 back, plus $5 of interest. But there's an issue- only $100 exists in total in the entire town's money supply! Even if you worked every job, and sold every product made in the town, (i.e., you created the entirety of the GDP), you would still only be able to scrounge up $100. The remaining $5 would never be repaid. The bank would put your loan into collections and try to seize your house in bankruptcy court- but it wouldn't matter. No matter what they do, the marginal $5 cannot be paid because IT DOES NOT EXIST. Thus, in order to prevent this paradox, the bank must go out and loan money to another person- their money will circulate in the economy, boosting money supply, and giving you the ability to earn the marginal $5 to pay your loan back. But again, the new borrower will run into the same situation in a year's time when the new loan comes due. They must again loan more money into the system than currently exists, to ensure that there is enough circulating supply to pay off existing loans.

This process repeats ad infinitum, perpetually compounding loan creation and thus money supply, in order to prevent systemic defaults. The system is BUILT for constant inflation. In the last 50 years, only about 12 quarters have seen reductions in commercial bank credit. That's less than 5% of the time. The other 95% has seen increases, per data from the St. Louis Fed.[67]

Even without accounting for debt crises, wars, and government defaults, money supply must therefore grow exponentially forever- solely in order to keep the wheels on the bus. The question is where that money supply goes- and herein lies the key to hyperinflation. In the aftermath of 2008, the Fed and Treasury worked together to purchase billions of dollars of troubled assets, mortgage backed securities, and Treasury bonds- all in a bid to halt the vicious deleveraging cycle that had frozen credit markets and already sunk two large investment banks. These programs were the most widespread and ambitious ever- and resulted in trillions of dollars of new money flowing into the financial system. Libertarian candidates and gold bugs such as Peter Schiff, who had rightly forecasted the Great Financial Crisis, now began to call for hyperinflation.

The trillions of printed money, he claimed, would create massive inflation that the government would not be able to tame. U.S. debt would be downgraded and sold, and with the Fed coming to the rescue with trillions more of QE, extreme money supply increases would ensue. An exponential growth curve in inflation was right around the corner. Gold prices rallied hard, moving from $855 at the start of 2008 to a record high of $1,970 by the end of 2011. The end of the world was upon us, many decried. Occupy Wall Street came out in force. However, to his great surprise, nothing happened. Inflation remained incredibly tame, and gold retreated from its euphoric highs. Armageddon was averted, or so it seemed. The issue that was not understood well at the time was that there existed two economies- the financial and the real. The Fed had pumped trillions into the financial economy, and with a global macroeconomic downturn plus foreign central banks buying Treasuries via dollar recycling, all this new money wasn't entering the real economy.

Instead, it was trapped, circulating in the hands of money market funds, equities traders, bond investors and hedge funds. The S&P 500, which had hit a record low in March of 2009, began a steady rally that would prove to be the strongest and most pronounced bull market in history. The Fed in the end did achieve extreme inflation- but only in assets. Without the Treasury incurring significant fiscal deficits this money did not flow out into the markets for goods and services but instead almost exclusively into equity and bond markets.

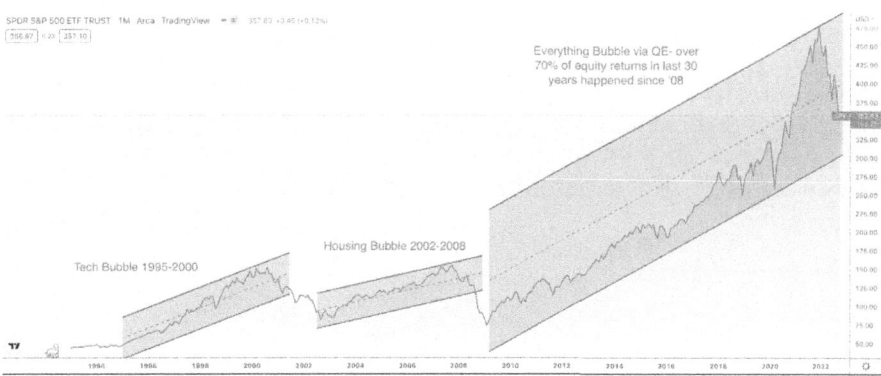

The great inflationary catastrophe touted by the libertarians and the gold bugs alike never came to pass- their doomsday predictions appeared frenetic, neurotic. Instead of re-evaluating their arguments under this new framework, the neo-Keynesians, who held the key positions of power with Treasury, the Federal Reserve, and most American universities (including my own) dismissed their ideas as economic drivel. The Fed had succeeded in averting disaster, or so they claimed. Bernanke, in all his infinite wisdom, had unleashed the "Wealth Effect"- a crucial behavioral economic theory suggesting that people spend more as the value of their assets rise. An even more extreme school of thought emerged- the Modern Monetary Theorists- who claimed that central banks had essentially discovered a 'perpetual motion machine'- a tool for unlimited economic growth as a result of zero bound interest rates and infinite QE. The government could borrow money indefinitely, and traditional metrics like Debt/GDP no longer mattered. Since each respective government could print money in their own currency- they could never default.

The bill would never be paid. Or so they thought.

The American Reckoning

This theory helped justify massive U.S. government borrowing and spending- from Afghanistan, to the War on Drugs, to Entitlement Programs, the Treasury indulged in fiscal largesse never before seen in our nation's history. The debt continued to accumulate and compound. With rates pegged at the zero bound, the Treasury could justify rolling the debt continually as the interest costs were minimal. Politicians now pushed for more and more deficit spending- if it's free to bailout the banks, or start a war- why not build more bridges? What about social programs? New Army bases? Tax cuts for corporations? Subsidies for businesses? There was no longer any "accepted" economic argument against this- and thus government spending grew and grew, and the deficits continued to expand year after year. The Treasury would roll the debt by issuing new bonds to pay off maturing ones- a strategy reminiscent of Ponzi schemes. This debt binge is accelerating- as spending increases, (and tax revenues are constant) the deficit grows, and this deficit is paid by more borrowing. This incurs more interest, and thus more spending to pay that interest, in a deadly feedback loop- what is called a debt spiral.[68]

The shadow threat here that is rarely discussed is unfunded liabilities- these are payments the Federal government has promised to make, but has not yet set aside the money for. This includes Social Security, Medicaid, Medicare, Veteran's benefits, and other funding that is non-discretionary, or in other words, basically non-optional. Cato Institute estimates that these obligations sum up to $163 trillion.[69] Other estimates from the Mercatus Center put the figure at between $87T as the lower bound and $222T on the high end.[70]

YES. That is TRILLION with a T.

A Dragon lurks in these shadows.

What makes it worse is that these figures are from 2012- the problem is significantly worse now. The fact of the matter is, no one knows the exact figure- just that it is so large it defies comprehension. These payments are what is called non-discretionary, or mandatory spending- each Federal agency is obligated to spend the money. They don't have a choice. Approximately 70% of all Federal spending is mandatory.[71] And the amount of mandatory spending is increasing each year as the Boomers, the second largest generation in American history, retire. Approximately 10,000 of them retire each day- increasing the deficits by hundreds of billions a year. Furthermore, the only way to cut these programs (via a bill introduced in the House and passed in the Senate) is basically political suicide. AARP and other senior groups are some of the most powerful and wealthy lobbying groups in the United States. If politicians don't have the stomach to legalize marijuana- an issue that Pew research finds an overwhelming majority of Americans supporting- then why would they nuke their own careers via cutting funding to seniors as inflation is rising?

Thus, although these obligations are not technically debt, they act as debt instruments in all other respects. The bill must be paid. In the Fiscal Report for 2022 released by the White House, they estimated that in 2021 and 2022 the Federal deficits would be $3.669T and $1.837T respectively.[72] This amounts to 16.7% and 7.8% of GDP (pg 42).

Table S–1. Budget Totals
(In billions of dollars and as a percent of GDP)

	2020	2021	2022	2023	2024	2025	2026	2027	2028	2029	2030	2031	Totals 2022-2026	Totals 2022-2031
Budget totals in billions of dollars:														
Receipts	3,421	3,581	4,174	4,641	4,826	5,038	5,332	5,632	5,888	6,119	6,370	6,643	24,013	54,665
Outlays	6,550	7,249	6,011	6,013	6,187	6,508	6,746	6,935	7,312	7,425	7,847	8,211	31,465	69,196
Deficit[1]	3,129	3,669	1,837	1,372	1,359	1,470	1,414	1,303	1,424	1,307	1,477	1,568	7,452	14,531
Debt held by the public	21,017	24,167	26,265	27,683	29,062	30,539	31,958	33,266	34,691	35,996	37,481	39,059		
Debt held by the public net of financial assets	18,024	21,684	23,520	24,892	26,250	27,720	29,134	30,437	31,860	33,167	34,643	36,216		
Gross domestic product (GDP)	21,000	22,030	23,500	24,563	25,537	26,516	27,533	28,590	29,697	30,867	32,094	33,391		
Budget totals as a percent of GDP:														
Receipts	16.3%	16.3%	17.8%	18.9%	18.9%	19.0%	19.4%	19.7%	19.8%	19.8%	19.8%	19.9%	18.8%	19.3%
Outlays	31.2%	32.9%	25.6%	24.5%	24.2%	24.5%	24.5%	24.3%	24.6%	24.1%	24.4%	24.6%	24.7%	24.5%
Deficit[1]	14.9%	16.7%	7.8%	5.6%	5.3%	5.5%	5.1%	4.6%	4.8%	4.2%	4.6%	4.7%	5.9%	5.2%
Debt held by the public	100.1%	109.7%	111.8%	112.7%	113.8%	115.2%	116.1%	116.4%	116.8%	116.6%	116.8%	117.0%		
Debt held by the public net of financial assets	85.8%	98.4%	100.1%	101.3%	102.8%	104.5%	105.8%	106.5%	107.2%	107.5%	107.9%	108.5%		
Memorandum, real net interest:														
Real net interest in billions of dollars	134	-53	-139	-189	-186	-138	-86	-36	9	50	108	164	-737	-442
Real net interest as a percent of GDP	0.6%	-0.2%	-0.6%	-0.8%	-0.7%	-0.5%	-0.3%	-0.1%	*	0.2%	0.3%	0.5%	-0.6%	-0.2%

*0.05 percent of GDP or less.
[1] The estimated deficit for 2021 is based on partial year actual data and generally incorporates actuals through March.

BUDGET OF THE U.S. GOVERNMENT FOR FISCAL YEAR 2022

Astonishingly, they project substantially decreasing deficits for the next decade. Meanwhile the U.S. is slowly grinding towards a severe recession (and then likely depression) as the Fed begins their tightening experiment into 132% federal debt to GDP. Deficits have basically never gone down in a recession, only up- unemployment insurance, food stamp programs, government initiatives; all drive the Treasury to pump out more money into the economy in order to stimulate demand and dampen any deflation. To add insult to injury, tax receipts collapse during recession- so the income side of the equation is negatively impacted as well. The budget will blow out. The U.S. 1 year Treasury bill is already trading at 4.7% as of November 2022- if we have to refinance our current debt loads at that rate (which we WILL since they have to roll the debt over), the Treasury will be paying $1.46 trillion in INTEREST ALONE YEARLY on the debt. That is equivalent to 40% of all Federal tax receipts in 2021!

I have tried to make the case that the United States is headed towards an "event horizon"- a point of no return, where the financial gravity of the supermassive debt is so crushing that nothing they do, short of Infinite QE, will allow us to escape.

The terrifying truth is that we are not headed towards this event horizon.

We're already past it.

As brilliant macro analyst Luke Gromen pointed out in several interviews late last year, if you combine Gross interest expense and entitlements, on a base case, we are already at 110% of tax receipts. True interest expense is now more than total Federal income. The Federal government is already bankrupt- the market just doesn't know it yet.

Luke Gromen speaking on the Macrovoices podcast, October 21st, 2021:[73]

"I think it also feeds into this being much more structurally inflationary than most people think, or many people think, is the fact that if you look at the US, what we call the US's true interest expense which we define as Treasury spending plus entitlement pay-goes, right the pay as you go portion of entitlements cause those are just the effective interest to support the entitlement obligations and you add those two numbers together. <u>What you find is that those two numbers are still 111% of US tax receipts as of the third quarter per the Treasury Borrowing Advisory Committee</u>. And that's with tax receipts at all time highs inflation by / aided by an epic everything bubble.

And so this, I think, is an element of the structural inflation that virtually nobody is talking about and I think it's something virtually everybody should be talking about, which is, everybody for 40 years has been conditioned that once we see these types of inflation, the Fed steps in to fight the inflation. <u>And the problem is, is that there have been no instances in the last 40 years, where the Fed has begun a tightening cycle, where the US couldn't even afford to pay its interest out of tax receipts</u>. And that's the case now, if we look at true interest expense, again, which is the Treasury spending plus entitlement pay goes, and so it leads to this conclusion that if the Fed tries to tighten, what you're likely going to see, before very long is a decline in tax receipts. If the Fed puts us in a recession, and we're already seeing significant slowing already. You're gonna be looking at tax receipts that are already below the true interest expense, and probably would start falling further, while the true interest expense would probably rise because of interest rates going up."

The black hole of debt, financed by the Federal Reserve, has now trapped the largest spending institution in the world, the United States Treasury. The unholy union of the money printer and the spender is catastrophic - the final key ingredient for monetary collapse.

This is How Money Dies.

The Dollar Endgame

True monetary collapses are hard to grasp for many in the West who have not experienced extreme inflation. The ever-increasing money printing seems strange, alien even. Why must money supply grow exponentially? Why did the Reichsbank continue printing even as hyperinflation took hold in Germany? Why did the Romans keep clipping coins as their economy collapsed? What is not understood well are the hidden feedback loops that dwell under the surface of the economy.

The Dragon of Inflation, once awoken, is near impossible to tame.

It all begins with a country walking itself into a situation of severe fiscal mismanagement- this could be the Roman Empire of the early 300s, or Germany in 1916, or America in the

2020s. The State, fighting a war, promoting a widescale welfare program, or combating an economic downturn, loads itself with debt burdens too heavy for it to bear. This might even create temporary illusions of wealth and prosperity. The immediate results are not felt. But the trap is laid. Over the next few years and even decades, the debt continues to grow. The government programs and spending set up during an emergency are almost impossible to shut down. Politicians are distracted with the issues of the day, and concerns about a borrowing binge take the backseat. The debt loads begin to reach a critical mass, almost always just as a political upheaval unfolds. Murphy's Law comes into effect.

Next comes a crisis.

This could be Visigoth tribesmen attacking the border posts in the North, making incursions into Roman lands. Or it could be the Assassination of Archduke Franz Ferdinand in Sarajevo, kicking off a chain of events causing the onset of World War 1. Or it could be a global pandemic, shutting down 30% of GDP overnight. Politicians respond as they always had- mass government mobilization, both in the real and financial sense, to address the issue. Promising that their solutions will remedy the problem, a push begins for massive government spending to "solve" economic woes. They go to fundraise debt to finance the

Treasury. But this time is different.

Very few, if any, investors bid. Now they are faced with a difficult question- how to make up for the deficit between the Treasury's income and its massive projected expenditure. Who's going to buy the bonds? With few or no legitimate buyers for their debt, they turn to their only other option- the printing press. Whatever the manner, new money is created and enters the supply.

Due to the flood of new liquidity entering the system, widespread inflation occurs. Confounded, the politicians blame everyone and everything but the printing as the cause. Bonds begin to sell off, which causes interest rates to rise. With rates suppressed so low for so long, trillions of dollars of leverage has built up in the system. No one wants to hold fixed income instruments yielding 1% when inflation is soaring above 8%. It's a guaranteed losing trade. As more and more investors run for the exits in the bond markets, liquidity dries up and volatility spikes. The MOVE index, a measure of bond market volatility, begins climbing to levels not seen since the 2008 Financial Crisis. Sovereign bond market liquidity begins to evaporate. Weak links in the system, overleveraged several times on government debt, such as the UK's pension funds, begin to implode.

The banks and Treasury itself will not survive true deflation-in the U.S., Yellen is already getting so antsy that she just asked major banks if Treasury should buy back their bonds to ensure liquidity![74] Demand for "risk free" debt is starting to decline. As yields rise, government borrowing costs spike and their ability to roll their debt becomes extremely impaired. Overleveraged speculators in housing, equity and bond markets begin to liquidate positions and a full-blown deleveraging event emerges. True deflation in a macro environment as indebted as ours would mean rates soaring well above 15-20%, and a collapse in money market funds, equities, bonds, and worst of all, a certain Treasury default as federal tax receipts decline, and deficits rise. A run on the banks would ensue. Without the Fed printing, the major banks, (which have a 0% capital reserve requirement since 3/15/20), would quickly be drained. Insolvency is not the only issue here- liquidity is; and without cash reserves a freezing of the interbank credit and repo markets would quickly ensue. For those who don't think this is possible, in the aftermath of Lehman Brothers' bankruptcy, McDonalds, Ford and GM were close to not making payroll or paying short term debt. They were worried that Bank of America would not roll their paper.[75]

As inflation rips higher, the $24 trillion Treasury market, and the $15.5 trillion corporate bond markets selloff hard. Soon they enter freefall as forced liquidations wipe leverage out of the system. Similar to 2008, credit markets begin to constrict lending. Thousands of "zombie corporations", firms held together only with razor thin margins and huge amounts of near zero yielding debt, begin to default. One study by a Deutsche analyst puts the figure at 25% of companies in the S&P 500.

The central banks respond to the crisis as they always have- coming to the rescue with the money printer, like the Bank of England did when they restarted QE in September 2022, or how the Bank of Japan began "emergency bond buying operations" a few months later.

But this time the liquidity wave is gargantuan. They have to print more than ever before as the entire debt based financial system unwinds. QE Infinity begins. Trillions of Treasuries, mortgage-backed securities, corporate bonds, and bond ETFs are bought up. The only manner in which to prevent the bubble from imploding is by overwhelming the system with freshly printed cash. Everything is no-limit bid. The tsunami of new money floods into the system and a face ripping rally begins in every major asset class. This is the beginning of the melt-up phase.

The Federal Reserve, within a few months, goes from owning

30% of the Treasury market, to 70% or more. The Bank of Japan is already at 70% ownership of certain JGB issuances, and some bonds haven't traded for a record number of days in an active market![76] The central banks EAT the bond market. The "Lender of Last Resort" becomes "The Lender of Only Resort".

Another step towards hyperinflation.
The Dragon crawls out of his lair.

Now the majority or even entirety of the new bond issuances from the Treasury are bought with printed money. Money supply must increase in tandem with federal deficits, fueling further inflation as more new money floods into the system. The Fed's liquidity hose is directly plugged into the veins of the real economy. The heroin of free money now flows in ever increasing amounts towards Main Street. The same face-ripping rise seen in equities in 2020 and 2021 is now mirrored in the markets for goods and services. Prices for food, gas, housing, computers, cars, healthcare, travel, and more explode higher. This sets off several feedback loops- the first of which is the wage-price spiral. As the prices of everything rise, real disposable income falls. Massive strikes and turnover ensues. Workers refuse to labor for wages that are not keeping up with their expenses. After much consternation, firms are forced to raise wages or see large scale work stoppages. These higher wages now mean the firm has higher costs, and thus must charge higher prices for goods. This repeats ad infinitum.

The next feedback loop is monetary velocity- the number of times one dollar is spent to buy goods and services per unit of time. If the velocity of money is increasing, then more transactions are occurring between individuals in an economy. The faster the dollar turns over, the more items it can bid for- and thus the more prices rise. Money velocity increasing is a key feature of a currency beginning to inflate away. In nations experiencing hyperinflation like Venezuela, where money velocity was purported to be over 7,000 annually- or more than 20 times a DAY.[77]

As prices rise steadily, people begin to increase their inflation expectations, which leads to them going out and preemptively buying before the goods become even more expensive. This leads to hoarding and shortages as select items get bought out quickly, and whatever is left is marked up even more. ANOTHER feedback loop.

Inflation now soars to 25%. Treasury deficits increase further as the government is forced to spend more to hire and retain workers, and government subsidies are demanded by every corner of the populace as a way to alleviate the price pressures. The government budget increases. Any hope of worker's pensions or banks buying the new debt is dashed as the interest rates remain well below the rate of inflation, and real wages continue to fall. They thus must borrow more as the entire system unwinds. The hyperinflationary feedback loop kicks in, with exponentially increasing borrowing from the Treasury matched by new money supply as the printer whirrs away.

The Dragon begins his fiery assault.

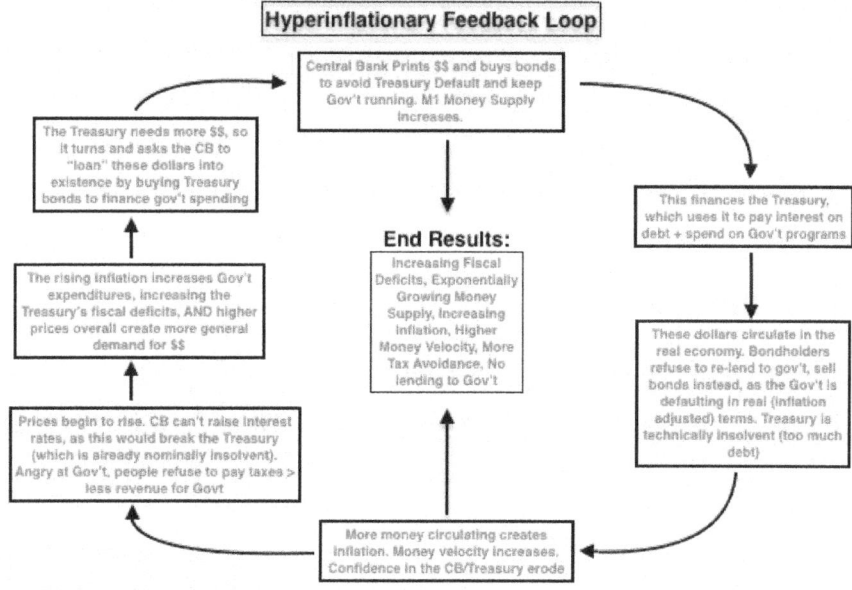

As the dollar devalues, other central banks continue printing furiously. This phenomenon of being trapped in a debt spiral is not unique to the United States- virtually every major economy is drowning under excessive credit loads, as the average G7 debt load is 135% of GDP.

As the central banks print at different speeds, massive dislocations begin to occur in currency markets. Nations who print faster and with greater debt monetization fall faster than others, but all fiats fall together in real terms. Global trade becomes extremely difficult. Trade invoices, which usually can take several weeks or even months to settle as the item is shipped across the world, go haywire as currencies move 20% or more against each other in short timeframes. Hedging becomes extremely difficult, as vol premiums rise and illiquidity is widespread.

Amidst the chaos, a group of nations comes together to decide to use a new monetary media- this could be the Special Drawing Right (SDR), a neutral global reserve currency created by the IMF. It could be a new commodity-based money, similar to how the U.S. dollar was originally pegged to gold. Or it could be Bitcoin, a peer-to-peer decentralized cryptocurrency with a hard supply limit and secure payment channels.

Whatever the case- it doesn't really matter. The dollar will begin to lose dominance as the world reserve currency as the new one arises.

As the old system begins to die, ironically the dollar soars higher on foreign exchange- as there is a $20 trillion global short position on the USD, in the form of leveraged loans, sovereign debt, corporate bonds, and interbank repo agreements. All this dollar debt creates dollar DEMAND, and if the U.S. is not printing fast enough or importing enough to push dollars out to satisfy demand, banks and institutions will rush to the forex market to dump their local currency in exchange for dollars. This drives DXY up even higher, and then forces more firms to dump local currency to cover dollar debt as the debt becomes more expensive, in a vicious feedback loop. This is called the Dollar Milkshake Theory, posited by Brent Johnson of Santiago Capital. The global Eurodollar market IS leverage- and as all leverage works, it must be fed with new dollars or risk bankrupting those who owe the debt. The fundamental issue is that this time, it is not banks, hedge funds, or even insurance giants- this is entire countries like Argentina, Vietnam, and Indonesia.

If the Fed does not print to satisfy the demand needed for this Eurodollar market, the Dollar Milkshake will suck almost all global liquidity and capital into the United States, which is a net importer and has largely lost its manufacturing base- meanwhile dozens of developing countries and manufacturing firms with dollar debts will go bankrupt and be liquidated, causing a collapse in global supply chains not seen since the Second World War. This would force inflation to rip above 50% as supply of goods collapses.

Worse yet, what will the Fed do? ALL their choices now make the situation worse.

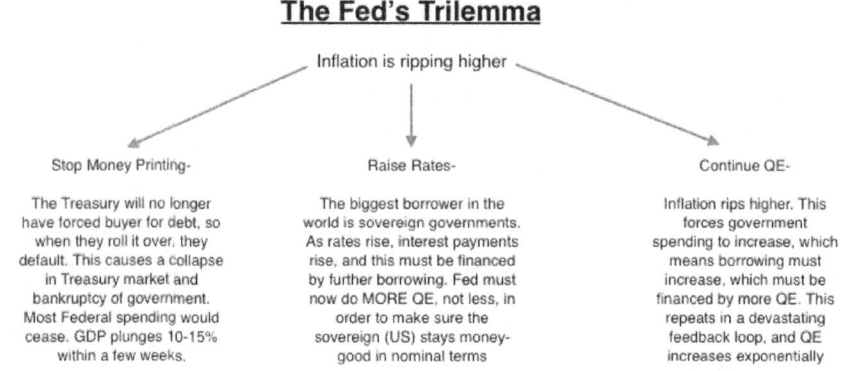

The Fed's Trilemma

Inflation is ripping higher

Stop Money Printing-	Raise Rates-	Continue QE-
The Treasury will no longer have forced buyer for debt, so when they roll it over, they default. This causes a collapse in Treasury market and bankruptcy of government. Most Federal spending would cease. GDP plunges 10-15% within a few weeks.	The biggest borrower in the world is sovereign governments. As rates rise, interest payments rise, and this must be financed by further borrowing. Fed must now do MORE QE, not less, in order to make sure the sovereign (US) stays money-good in nominal terms	Inflation rips higher. This forces government spending to increase, which means borrowing must increase, which must be financed by more QE. This repeats in a devastating feedback loop, and QE increases exponentially

Many pundits will retort- "Even if we have to print the entire unfunded liability of the US, $160 trillion, that's 8 times current M2 Money Supply. So we'd see 700% inflation over a few years or even decades, which is manageable, and then it would be over!"

This is a grave misunderstanding of the problem; as the Fed expands money supply and finances Treasury spending, inflation rips higher, forcing the AMOUNT THE TREASURY SPENDS, AND THUS THE AMOUNT THE FED PRINTS in the next fiscal quarter to increase! Thus a 100% increase in money supply can cause a 150% increase in inflation, and on again, and again, ad infinitum.

M2 Money Supply increased 41% since March 5th, 2020, and

we saw an 18% realized increase in inflation (not CPI, which is manipulated) and a 58% increase in the S&P 500 (at the top). This was with the majority of printed money really going into the financial markets, and only stimulus checks and transfer payments flowing into the real economy. Now federal deficits are increasing, and in the next easing cycle, the Fed will be buying the majority of Treasury bonds. The next $10 trillion they print, therefore, could cause additional inflation requiring another $15 trillion of printing. This could cause another $25 trillion in money printing; this cycle continues forever, like Weimar Germany discovered.

The $200 trillion or so they need to print to finance the unfunded liabilities can easily multiply into the quadrillions by the time we get there.

The Inflation Dragon consumes all in his path.

Federal Net Outlays are currently around 30% of GDP. Of course, the government has tax receipts that it could use to pay for services, but as prices roar higher, the real value of government tax revenue falls. At the end of the Weimar hyperinflation, tax receipts represented less than 1% of all government spending. This means that without Treasury spending, literally a third of all economic output would cease. The holders of dollar debt begin dumping them en masse for assets with real world utility and value- even simple things such as food and gas.

People will be forced to ask themselves- what matters more; the amount of Apple shares they hold or their ability to buy food next month? The option will be clear- and as they sell, massive flows of money will move out of the financial economy and into the real. This begins the final cascade of money into the marketplace which causes the prices of everything to soar higher. The demand for money grows even larger as prices spike, which causes more Treasury spending, which must be financed by new borrowing, which is printed by the Fed. The final doom loop begins, and money supply explodes exponentially. Monetary velocity rips higher and eventually pushes inflation into the thousands of percent. Goods begin being re-priced by the day, and then by the hour, as the value of the currency becomes meaningless. A new money, most likely a cryptocurrency such as Bitcoin, gains widespread adoption- becoming the preferred method and eventually the default payment mechanism. The State continues attempting to force the citizens to use their currency- but by now all trust in the money has collapsed. The only thing that works is force, but even the police, military and legal system by now have completely lost confidence.

The Simulacrum breaks down as the masses begin to realize that the entire financial system, and the very currency that underpins it is a lie- an illusion, propped up via complex derivatives, unsustainable debt loads, and easy money financed by the central banks. Similar to Weimar Germany, confidence in the currency finally collapses as the public awakens to a long-forgotten truth-

There is no supply cap on fiat currency.

When asked in 2020 if there was a limit to the Fed's ability to print money and flood the system with cash, Neel Kashkari, president of the Federal Reserve Bank of Minneapolis responded:

"There is no end to our ability to do that."[78]

All fiat money systems, unmoored from the tethers of hard money, are now adrift in a sea of illusion, of make-believe. The only fundamental props to support it are the trust and network effects of the participants.

These are powerful forces, no doubt- and have made it so no fiat currency dies without severe pain inflicted on the masses, most of which are uneducated about the true nature of economics and money. But the Ships of State have wandered into a maelstrom from which there is no return. Currently, total worldwide debt stands at a gargantuan $300 trillion, equivalent to 356% of global GDP.[79]

This means that even at low interest rates, interest expense will be higher than GDP- we can never grow our way out of this trap, as many economists hope. Fiat systems demand ever increasing debt, and ever-increasing money printing, until the illusion breaks and the flood of liquidity is finally released into the real economy. Financial and Real economies merge in one final crescendo that dooms the currency to die, as all fiats must.

Day by day, hour by hour, the interest accrues.

The debt grows larger.

And the Dollar Endgame approaches.

ADDENDUM

I wrote this section as purely a response to the hundreds of questions, comments, and rebuttals I received over this series. They are listed in no particular order, and I do my best to answer each point as concisely and accurately as possible.

QE is not money printing! QE is the creation of bank reserves which are swapped for commercial bank assets within the financial system.

Ok, a lot to unpack here. First, in a technical sense you are correct; QE does not create money in the form that normal people think of as money. No physical cash is printed and shipped to banks, instead the Fed "prints" by adding entries to their internal SQL ledger and exchanges these new entries for assets. These entries are bank reserves, and like I have already described, are exchanged for assets, mostly Treasuries. They can't be immediately "spent" into the real economy- they are a form of money, but they are trapped exclusively in the financial system, within the markets. Joseph Wang, former senior trader at the Federal Reserve, describes this best, explaining that we have a two-tiered money system- the bank reserves trapped at the Fed, and commercial bank deposits that the rest of us can access.[80] These two systems interact and work with each other to provide liquidity and funding. This doesn't disprove the Dollar Endgame hypothesis- because they can be turned into real economy dollars through the Treasury. Therefore high fiscal deficits are the key to extreme inflation- it's a pairing of the money PRINTER with the money SPENDER.

When the Treasury issues bonds, they receive funds as consideration in the form of commercial bank deposits. These commercial bank deposits turn into a deposit at the Treasury General Account (TGA) and absolutely CAN be spent in the real economy! Or else what is the point of all this? Why would the government issue debt for money it cannot spend on real world essentials like tanks, bridges, pensions or hospitals?

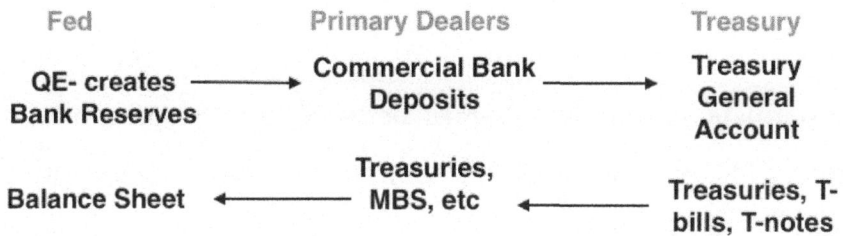

Through this process, the banking system and Treasury paired together turn bank reserves, which can only be held by commercial banks at the Fed, into deposits, and then into funds in the Treasury General Account, which can now be spent in the REAL economy. The Treasury is the missing link- which is why in 2008 we didn't see widespread inflation, because the massive tsunami of QE was trapped within the financial system and could not be spent in the real world. We saw inflation in financial assets, but nothing else. Once the Treasury is underwater and is continually incurring significant fiscal deficits, and the Fed is monetizing these deficits through QE, that is when we see a massive increase in inflation and a resurgence of the vicious feedback loops that propelled countries like Weimar Germany to monetary doom and hyperinflation.

The true risk is deflation, not inflation. Macro indicators point to a global recession on a scale not seen since 2008. The Fed will hike us out of inflation.

I am not surprised that many believe this, as all mainstream economists in the late 1960's believed that stagflation was impossible, or that the dollar could never de-peg from gold. Of course, the macro indicators point towards deflation- central banks are hiking rates into 356% global debt to GDP, oncoming recession, energy crises, and war. However, what you and many others completely fail to understand is the entire point of the central banks.

They do not exist to "maximize" employment.
They do not exist to "minimize" inflation.
They exist to backstop the banks, markets, and most of all, the federal governments via money printing.

They care about "financial stability" more than anything- to them, this means the Treasury has enough cash to roll over its debt, and the banks have enough cash to meet redemptions. Just look at their actions! Honestly, who cares what they proclaim their motives to be. Every time there is a financial crisis, they find another excuse, another reason, to turn the money printer back on. Do you really think that if the Treasury defaults on its debts, and all Treasury bonds enter freefall, that they're going to sit back and do nothing? They have printed trillions for far less.

Treasuries are the backbone of the global financial system. They are used as collateral in the Eurodollar market, they are held by sovereign wealth funds, used to support forex currency pegs, and most importantly fund the largest military superpower the world has ever seen. The Treasury rate is used throughout finance- described as the "risk free rate" ; they are used in almost every valuation metric, including Option Pricing Models, Backsolves, GPCs, DCFs, etc. I would know- this is the industry I work in!

The importance of this asset cannot be understated. The Fed will do anything to prevent a deflationary collapse- and they will have to print, as we have already covered, the U.S. Treasury is already bankrupt, deep underwater with $31 trillion of Federal Debt, and $163T of unfunded liabilities. To prevent a bankruptcy, the Fed will print WHATEVER IT TAKES. This money will be spent in the real economy, as fiscal deficits are at all time highs, and inflation will spike higher, even as the economy contracts while the Fed continues hiking. Just look at Argentina- they have 83% inflation, and they have 75% interest rates! They are hiking all they can and it does nothing. It all leads back to a tweet I wrote a while ago-

"Peruvian Bull's debt paradox: the more the Fed hikes, the more interest on the nat'l debt rises, the closer Treasury moves to insolvency. Which means the closer the Fed comes

to restarting QE. The higher they hike, the farther they move behind the curve. No. Way. Out"

So no, the Fed hiking will not lead to widespread deflation- the Treasury will break before that happens, and the system will be flooded with money. Ironically the higher and faster they hike, the quicker the largest borrowers in the world, the federal governments themselves, become bankrupt. We are in a macro environment that is more indebted than any other time in human history. The higher they raise rates, the more interest is due on all these debts, and to prevent a collapse greater than the Great Depression, the central banks have to print MORE. Thus hiking rates ironically really does nothing in the long term to fix the situation. It may slow inflation in the short term but it dooms the central bank to print more in the long run in order to stave off Treasury collapse.

All this inflation is caused by corporate greed. Large companies with monopolies are hiking prices to take advantage. It's all a scam.

Look, I completely understand where this is coming from. A ton of corporations have taken advantage of their market share to hike prices, garner unfair profits, and even fire workers without cause. This much is true. However, the broad increase in prices of everything, from lumber, to coal, to computers and food, is not due to soulless companies- it is due to a 40% rise in M2 money supply financed by the Fed! Milton Friedman said it best- "Inflation is always and everywhere a monetary phenomenon, in the sense that it is and can be produced only by a more rapid increase in the quantity of money than in output."

Restaurants, small businesses, real estate, family farms, plumbing companies, and many more distributed industries saw large increases in prices charged to consumers in the last 2 years- this is without major monopolies controlling the majority stake! And for those who would posit that this inflation is "just due to the war in Ukraine" and gas disruptions from Russia, may I remind you that inflation was already at 7.5% per the BLS in January 2022, before the war had even begun![81]

It's easy to blame businesses for this phenomenon, and like I stated- there are definitely some firms guilty of price gouging consumers and calling it inflation. But your local small deli store or carpentry shop aren't raising prices to hurt you, they're doing so because the price of all their inputs are rising- and thus what they charge to consumers must rise as well.

If deflationary collapse occurs or the government defaults, we can repeat

the Bernanke playbook post 2008; just lower interest rates again to 0% to ensure Treasury solvency.

This is a common counterargument. However, it falls prey to the exact same conundrum that was discussed earlier- namely how everything the Fed does to avert disaster would make the situation worse, not better. By lowering interest rates to 0%, this stimulates loan demand and therefore credit creation, which spurs an increase in money supply as the banks lend money into existence. Everyone goes to take out loans, buying cars, houses, food and essentials on credit. Debt burden thus increases in the system overall, making it even harder for the Fed to raise rates in the future. And this serves to incentivize the Treasury to borrow and spend even more recklessly, as they have the excuse of low interest rates to finance government spending. ALL this does is only slightly delay the inevitable and in the end make the problem worse, not better.

Furthermore, this credit boom increases inflation as new money is created and pumped into the system. So, it doesn't even solve that problem. The fundamental issue, stated again and again, is that the Treasury is underwater and is spending out the wazoo, and as inflation continues to rise, Treasury spending will continue to rise and thus borrowing will increase. Lastly, let's talk about the elephant in the room- the bond market!! If the

Fed implements Yield Curve Control, similar to what the Bank of Japan did to their market, then they would effectively push bond yields down, but the price would be promising to do infinite QE to buy any bond with a yield above the set amount. Who wants to buy 0%, or 0.5% bonds, when inflation is 8%? Nobody- so the Fed will have to be the buyer of only resort, which means they will effectively monetize all Federal deficit spending. QE will thus steadily increase for the foreseeable future as the entire bond market gets eaten by the Fed.

Money velocity is insanely low and keeps dropping, thus inflation will subside back to 2% within a year or so.

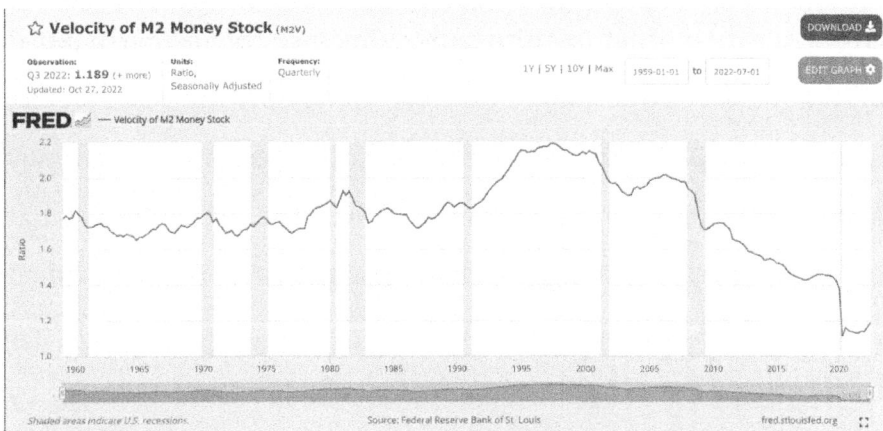

This is another common argument, especially among those who are educated in economics. At first glance they seem correct, as the chart above from the Fed demonstrates.[82] There appears to have been a massive collapse in money velocity since the late 1990s and especially since COVID. What they fail to understand is that the manner in which money velocity is calculated is extremely flawed. Instead of using the actual transaction volume of the economy divided by GDP (which would be difficult to do, but could potentially be done with data from Visa and Mastercard as well as ATM txs), they calculate it as

"the ratio of quarterly nominal GDP to the quarterly average of M2 money stock."

Thus, the denominator is the money supply- and as money supply expands, the equation forces "money velocity" lower and lower. This equation works well enough if you have stable GDP growth and flat or miniscule money supply growth; but it blows out as soon as we see massive money printing like we did in 2008 or 2020. The estimate therefore goes lower as money supply increases, which is ironically just the opposite of what happens in reality! Just take this equation to the real world- if countries like Venezuela who have hyperinflation suddenly use this metric, they would theoretically reduce money velocity by printing more money. The velocity there, with money supply growth over 5000% YoY, could easily approach infinitely near zero, what is called in mathematics an asymptote. This function would be estimating that 1 Venezuelan bolivar only changes hands every century, or less. If you go in the streets or talk to the people living under this monetary hellscape, you will see that they spend every dollar the day they get paid- as prices will change hour to hour, day to day. They treat their currency like melting ice cubes in the hot tropical sun; they must be used immediately or else be completely wasted. These kinds of illogical, nonsensical equations can only be thought of in the ivory towers of academia and banking institutions which are protected from the consequences of the real world. None of this works in practice.

So no, money velocity didn't really fall THAT far in 2020, it just appears that way due to the way it is calculated. Now, did it fall somewhat, maybe 10-20%?? Sure! But that can only be surmised by looking at live transaction data on the real economy, not arcane equations made up by the Fed.

So many PHDs and so little common sense....

QE is a net good for the economy. It creates a wealth effect and thus stimulates aggregate demand, increasing prosperity and asset prices for all. The rising tide lifts the boats.

This is another common argument I see from the Neo-

Keynesians. Let's remember first that QE is a completely new experiment- it was not used during the 1800s and early 1900s for example, where America entered the Gilded Age and experienced some of the fastest economic growth in human history. It wasn't used during the 1950s or 60s, another period of rapid development. So we were able to achieve massive economic growth without centralized banking or money printing- in fact, I would argue that on a percent of GDP basis we grew faster during these times and the average worker experienced far more prosperity than now. It's only been used at scale post the 2008 financial crisis and into the "lost decade" of the 2010s and 2020s that we are currently experiencing. The thesis was by boosting asset prices we therefore boost the economy; but this is asinine on several levels. First, who holds the assets? Recall that the top 10% of Americans hold 84% of all registered stocks on exchanges. They also hold the majority of the land, housing, businesses, and debt instruments. Goosing asset prices higher only directly helps these economic elites- it does little for everyone else.

Besides, this creates the "credit boom" that Mises described- an artificial rise in asset prices solely due to central bank interference. It is not based on true economic productivity. The Fed creates no new factories, they create no new jobs, no innovations, no startups. Instead they create cheap money which "funds" these things- but as the price of money gets distorted, so do investments, and thus unprofitable and useless projects are built up with debt.

This results in a phenomenon similar to the Chinese "ghost cities"- entire sections of the economy built without need or purpose, and worse, they waste limited commodities and energy to create. When the debt cycle rolls over, as it always does, the debt must be paid, and the assets that are liquidated are found to be near worthless- a waste of time, energy and resources.

QE therefore harms the real economy and enriches the wealthy at the same time. It cannot be said to be capitalist or socialist; it is simply plutocracy and kleptocracy; crony capitalism where the wealthy steal from the poor and foot them with the bill.
Even if inflation gets a bit high, it won't and can't get worse. The system will be fine, and the Fed hikes will cure the situation. It'll be rocky for a little bit, similar to the stagflation of the 1970s, but we'll get through this and in a few years it'll be back to 2%, no problem. The issue with this argument is one of scale. Sure, in the late 1970s and early 1980s, the Fed, under the reign of Volcker, was able to hike rates to the 20% range, but debt to GDP at the time was 30%- not the mammoth 132% we have now.

Besides, this doesn't take into effect the slippage that will occur in bond markets- as the Fed continues to hike, bonds will sell off hard, racing ahead of the Fed and moving rates much higher, much faster than the Fed anticipates. With $31 trillion of Federal debt, this means interest expense will spike; thus the Treasury must borrow more to rollover existing debt and in doing so lock in higher coupon payments, OR they must ask the Fed to pin interest rates low, in a policy called Yield Curve Control. However, this requires infinite QE as every time the yields peek their head above the target interest rate, the central bank must print as much money as needed to buy bonds, forcing rates back down to the target. The Bank of Japan is currently experimenting with this policy, and it is creating an emerging markets currency crisis for them. Besides, this ignores the basic feedback loops that take place once inflation rises above 2 or 3%- first, the inflation expectations loop, where people frontload purchases, driving up prices. Next is the Treasury feedback loop- more inflation means deficit spending increases, which means more government borrowing, which means more QE, which means more inflation.

After that is money velocity- as inflation increases and people lose faith in the currency the speed of transacting in the money starts to increase. This increases inflation as the dollars get turned over faster, and are able to bid more products within a given timeframe (say a month or a year). Next is the wage price spiral, where prices rise, forcing workers to strike or demand higher pay, which is usually eventually given, which increases business costs, which forces higher prices, repeating the feedback loop. Long story short, once the inflation genie is out of the bottle, it is very hard to put back- and it usually begins to grow a life of its own. These processes feed on each other exponentially. Worse yet, like already stated, there is $31 trillion of federal debt, $20 trillion or so of Eurodollar debt overseas, and $166-$222 trillion of unfunded liabilities owed by the U.S. government - all debts which must be paid in dollars, which must either be paid through taxation or the printing press. Passing new tax laws during an economic downturn is essentially political suicide, so the printing press is the likeliest answer here.

The REAL risk for hyperinflation lies in the international community finding another world reserve currency - if this happens, either slowly or over time, the global demand for dollars switches into global supply of dollars as USD positions are liquidated in favor of the new global reserve currency. The dollars are now dumped for real goods and services- and the strong tailwind of demand becomes a headwind of supply as USDs flood back into America, bidding up prices of land, food, manufactured goods etc. The scramble becomes a stampede and the entire system unwinds as trillions of dollars flow back to the States, causing a massive whiplash in inflation and further pushing the U.S. Treasury into deficit spending, thus causing more money creation, and more inflation, in a vicious feedback loop. Again, this process may take years to play out- but no reserve currency has lasted forever, and the inherent structural defects explained by Triffin's Dilemma cannot resolve themselves. All currencies come to an end.

What would the effect of a CBDC (Central Bank Digital Currency) be? Would it be able to be used to "reset" the system?

I am being completely honest and transparent when I say this- CBDCs must be resisted at all costs. Most people are completely blind to the level of Orwellian control that this sort of technology would implement over the populace. Remember, Keynesian economic theory rests on stimulating spending and consumption, and utilizing government deficits and central bank money printing to pull economies out of depressions. It arose from a need to get the U.S. and Britain out of their 1930's economic contraction and into a strong economic position in order to fight World War II. The Keynesians believed the best way to stimulate spending would be to cause inflation, as this would force people with "hoards of cash under their mattress" to go out and spend these funds before they lost more value. There was no way to centrally force people to spend- they could just increase money supply and pump that money into the economy by government spending in order to hike inflation up and as a second order effect, produce higher spending patterns.

They've always wanted more control over spending- and a CBDC would get them there. With a CBDC, they would eliminate the need to have banks, credit unions or trust companies- you would essentially just make a direct account with the Fed. The Fed would be able to create new policies, written in code, that would enforce certain actions on your deposits. They could program in a 1% weekly negative interest rate- the balance would decline by 1% a week in perpetuity, and thus you would be forced to spend or invest it unless you wanted to see your money disappear. They could enforce taxes directly to your account. You buy cigarettes? That's unhealthy and against their guidelines. $15 taken. Alcohol? Doesn't promote work ethic- $10. New car? That's bad for the environment. $1900.

They could even ban travel, remove the ability to buy firearms or food, and reduce your ability to use healthcare services. The issue is not whether these things are good or bad- there are arguments to be made for reducing consumption, buying used cars, reducing environmental waste, etc. The issue is that to force these policies on the people via a CBDC would grant the Fed and Treasury virtually unlimited, Orwellian power to control and command almost every aspect of a citizen's life. Freedom of speech would now be an afterthought- who cares about the protest if no one can buy a bus ticket, Uber, or gas to get there? The worst thing is these extreme neo-Keynesian economists actually this would be a good thing! "Think of all the policies we could implement! We could ban smoking, we could reduce travel, we could lower CO_2 emissions directly! We could even eliminate the IRS as we can tax people directly from their bank account!" In my opinion, the economists who support these kinds of policies are nothing but grifters, frauds and cronies of the lowest sort- those willing to force total financial control on the populace so that their "theories" can be tried in real time, on real people.

Furthermore, I think it would be incredibly difficult for them to "reset" the system. Monetary resets have happened before, but usually they occur only under the most difficult and strenuous of circumstances, and involve an issuance of a new currency that is some fraction of the old one- for example, in Peru, due to the bad state of economy and hyperinflation in the late 1980s, the government was forced to abandon the inti and introduce the sol as the country's new currency. The sol, a new currency, was introduced in Peru on July 1, 1991, through Law No. 25,295. It replaced the inti at a rate of 1 sol to 1,000,000 intis. Coins denominated in the new currency were made available on October 1, 1991, and the first banknotes were released on November 13, 1991. The introduction of the sol was essentially a "reverse stock split" of the old currency, meant to increase confidence in the currency, stabilize bank deposits, slow down the circulation of money, and reduce inflation. The "reset" would likely hurt the working class the most- as some wealthy government elites would know about it beforehand, they would sell their assets for another currency, wait until the conversion, and then re-buy the assets with the new currency. The old currency, the Inti, quickly became completely useless as everyone switches to the new system. I'll be honest, I'm not exactly sure what a CBDC "reset" would look like, as it has never been tried before. I think the main issue is the debt- does the debt get converted as well? If so, then the problem may not be really solved. If you convert the debt at 10:1 and the currency at 10:1, what has really changed?

Nothing- and therefore likely what they would do is apply a different conversion rate to debt to de-lever the system and wipe at least some of it out. But this is all speculation.
CBDCs must be resisted. At all costs.

Just cut government spending down to zero, or close to it! This would solve the issue.

This is another common counterargument- the hyperinflationary feedback loop rests on government deficit spending, which increases during inflation, resulting in more borrowing, and thus more money printing, and thus more inflation. If we cut government spending enough to drastically reduce deficits, we would essentially be gutting our own economy, and very quickly bring on a Great Depression. The only "tool" that we have to escape a Great Depression quickly IS government spending, and thus we would be in for a long, hard downturn with severe unemployment and price collapse.

Remember the equation for GDP:

$$Y = C + I + G + (X-M)$$

Where;

Y= National Income (GDP)

C= Consumer Spending

I= Investment

G= Government Spending

X= Exports

M= Imports

Government spending is part of the value add of the formula FOR GDP. Thus, if we reduce government spending, all else being equal, we REDUCE GDP. According to data from the St. Louis

Fed, Federal Net Outlays are currently 29% of GDP, in 2021 data. Thus, if we were to severely slash government spending, we would see a reduction of 25% or so. To get rid of the deficits, we would have to slash so much spending that we would basically immediately see a collapse of 16% of GDP within a few weeks.

As all things do in economics, this would have immediate knock- on effects. Government contractors, like Boeing, Lockheed Martin, or Raytheon would quickly lose huge revenue streams. Massive layoffs would occur across defense, infrastructure, social services, and more- and within a few months GDP would drop another 10% or so. This would spur on a deflationary wave similar to the Great Depression. Unemployment would soar- bringing all the issues with it, the soup lines, homelessness, crime, collapsing house and business values, and political upheaval. If the FDIC did not step in to print enough money to shore up the banks, there would be widespread bank runs as the capital reserve requirement for banks is 0%- and most banks only hold 2-5% of reserves in cash to pay out to consumers who want to redeem their deposits. In my opinion, all this is besides the point- the government will NEVER cut spending this much, and create this severe of a depression, to stave off a crisis they believe cannot occur.

Firstly, most government spending is mandatory- per the

Government Accountability Office, 70% of federal outlays are already earmarked and must be spent.[83] To reduce the size of these programs would basically require an act of Congress, a bill passing through the House and Senate and signed by the President. The other 30% of discretionary spending is very hard to cut as well- lobbyists, corporations, citizen's rights groups, unions, and other powerful interests will do anything in their power to ensure that the money continues to flow into their coffers. Besides, some of these programs are good, or at least appear good! Imagine the political backlash if a House Rep proposes to cut food stamp benefits, or funding for the DEA, or National Parks Service. Remember who runs our country- and these people will do virtually anything to prevent the money spigot from turning off. They do not believe, or maybe don't even care, if extreme inflation comes. They are benefiting from the structure of the current system- why would they change it?

Delete all the debt!

The basic equation learned in first year finance and accounting programs is this:

$$A = L + OE$$

Where;

A= Assets

L= Liabilities

OE= Owners Equity

Thus, for every asset there is a liability or equity. If you destroy one side of the equation, the liability side, you simultaneously destroy the other side of the equation, on someone else's balance sheet! Treasury bonds are debt, and a lot of them are held by Boomers in retirement accounts. Even if we could go in and somehow "delete" the bonds and annul the coupon payments, this would be tantamount to deleting assets of these retirees- and what will they have to retire with then? The retirement accounts would lose trillions of dollars' worth of value!There is no easy way out of this trap. Remember, in a debt based monetary system, most money is actually credit- the only "real" money that is not someone else's liability is cash, but his makes up for less than 6% of total money supply. Imagine if we had a 94% reduction in money supply within a few months- the pure economic catastrophe that would occur is unimaginable.

Besides, recall that debt-based instruments, like Treasury bonds, are literally the collateral that holds this whole system up. There is $2.2T in reverse repo secured by Treasuries, and most of the Eurodollar market, as well as the interbank repo market (which blew up in September 2019, spurring a Fed rescue). Wiping out the debt would also wipe out the collateral which underlies the entire financial system. It's all intricately linked together, like a wired bomb- remove any connection, and the whole thing can blow. That's not to say that this would be impossible, just that it is very unlikely to be taken as a serious response to the crisis.

Deflation is the easy way out. The people in charge will see the inflationary crisis coming and opt for a de-leveraging of the system instead.

Again, I wish I could say I believed this would be the case. First thing you have to understand, a deflationary crisis would be better and worse than an inflationary crisis in different ways. We would see a complete collapse of the asset bubbles in stocks, bonds, real estate, technology, crypto, art, and more as the leverage in the system unwinds. There would be massive layoffs as government subsidized industries grind to a halt, and a collapse in GDP as huge parts of the federal government, defense and infrastructure sectors, and transfer payments like social security completely turn off. The public backlash from this would be incredible- a new Occupy Wall Street, and severe protests from people across the political spectrum over the defaulted promises of the government. Unemployment could easily soar to 20% or more. Bread and soup lines, homelessness, crime, and more would proliferate. Bank runs would occur, and if the FDIC did not get Treasury or Fed backing, their cash on hand would run out and bank deposits would no longer be insured. Your money in the bank would become worthless.

Money market funds, hedge funds, pension funds- all would collapse. Only those who hold physical cash would fare well; as prices of everything enter freefall, they could rush in and buy distressed assets at bargain prices. Overall, would this be better for the working class than hyperinflation? Probably. Most debts, including credit card, auto loans, student loans, and mortgages would default, and the banks, unable to collect the tsunami of assets that they are "owed" as collateral, would likely fail. The system only works on the margins- if a few people default on mortgages, the banks can repossess their homes and sell them. What if the majority default? Police would likely not be willing to go door to door through entire neighborhoods and kick residents out for a greedy bank that over levered itself and will fail without these assets.

Besides, remember who runs the system- the wealthy, by and large. They own most of the assets; the land, the casinos, the businesses, the stocks, bonds, and derivatives. The system unwinding and asset prices collapsing means a collapse of THEIR wealth more than anyone else's. The notion that they would opt for this depressionary outcome rather than an inflationary one, which is comparatively better for them, is asinine.

What if you're wrong? These predictions are extreme, and others have predicted this before. It didn't happen.

I don't think I'm wrong, but even if I am, I think the bull case is a worse version of the 1970s stagflation. Inflation is already at 8%, via official CPI data (realized inflation is probably already around 16%). Stagflation, for reference, is an economic condition whereby the economy contracts while inflation remains elevated. Layoffs are already becoming widespread, especially in the tech, auto and mortgage industries, which have the most sensitivity to rising interest rates. Oil prices are exacerbating the inflation situation- energy is the input to virtually every single moving part of our economy, and thus higher energy prices means higher and more sustained inflation rates. We are having record inflation while the US is draining the Strategic Petroleum Reserve (SPR) and while China is offline. In a Macrovoices interview in October 2022, Louis Vincent Gave laid out the case that when China comes back online, they will require an additional 1.5M barrels per day of oil, which will likely shoot prices back above the $120 level, from the $80 or so they are at now. This could shoot inflation easily above 10%.

Payrolls have been stronger than expected, but I believe this is mainly due to declines in full time positions and increases in part time positions. The U.S. economy will fare relatively well for the next year or so compared to other countries given the built in demand for the dollar, but in my opinion if the Fed continues hiking we will see a severe recession, and eventually depression if they go high enough.

Tax the rich at 100% and that will cure the issue

If we tax all the billionaires at 100% we would acquire roughly $4.18T worth of assets.[84] However, there is a gargantuan $31T of debt and $160T to $222T of unfunded liabilities. This would be a drop in the bucket. Furthermore, a LOT of these assets are illiquid, hard to value, or dependent on market conditions. If the Treasury somehow acquired 20% of Tesla, for example, they could only sell small amounts slowly so that they do not crush the market and shoot themselves in the foot. Even if we take it at face value, $4.18 trillion would only pay for about 8 months of Federal spending (using 2021 figures). The issue is just too big for even the wealthiest to handle. The politicians have dug us a hole so deep that it is impossible to get out.

What will replace the Dollar as World Reserve Currency?

This is an incredibly difficult question to answer, as there is great uncertainty surrounding how the major powers will react to an unwind of the dollar-centric global monetary system. The last few times we had a transition to a new world reserve currency, there was a clear rising global superpower that could take on the mantle and conduct enough trade to keep the system running. For example, the most recent transition occurred from 1929-1944 took a decade and half, and required serious damage to the former global superpower, Great Britain. Pulling every resource to slow the German onslaught in the early stages of World War II, Churchill was increasingly worried of the potential of a mass invasion of the home island, and thus began shipping British gold to the United States to be stored with the Fed and Treasury for safekeeping. Other Allied nations, such as France, followed suit. Hundreds of tons of gold flowed west- and by the end of the war the US had 50% of the above ground gold in the world. Standing virtually untouched by the ravages of war, while Europe and Asia lay devastated, America superseded Great Britain in terms of military and economic strength.

She was now able to lay the terms of global trade- with the only Navy large enough to protect vital trade routes from state actors and pirates, the U.S. could now force her own terms on the world, and these terms were cemented in the Bretton Woods agreement in 1944. The dollar would now be the new world reserve currency- and instead of holding gold and trading gold certificates, they would hold dollars, which would be redeemable for gold. This system worked because there was one superpower with sufficient might to enforce it- but after a breakdown in our current monetary system, there is no single nation that can become a lone hegemon.

China has a closed capital account- they don't really allow free movement of capital out of the country, which has to be done if you want to have a reserve currency. India does not have a navy large enough to enforce trade. Russia is a massive commodities powerhouse, but has a declining population, crumbling infrastructure, and as we have seen in Ukraine, a military that is far more of a paper tiger than most analysts had predicted. There is no unipolar world in our future- only a multipolar one, with various regional powers vying for control. In this sort of a system, the new reserve currency would have to be a neutral one. There are several different options.

The first is something called the Special Drawing Right, or SDR. The International Monetary Fund's website describes it like this:[85]

"The SDR is an international reserve asset, created by the IMF in 1969 to supplement its member countries' official reserves. The SDR was created as a supplementary international reserve asset in the context of the Bretton Woods fixed exchange rate system. The collapse of the Bretton Woods system in 1973 and the shift of major currencies to floating exchange rate regimes lessened the reliance on the SDR as a global reserve asset. Nonetheless, SDR allocations can play a role in providing liquidity and supplementing member countries' official reserves, as was the case amid the global financial crisis.

The SDR serves as the unit of account of the IMF and other international organizations. The SDR is neither a currency nor a claim on the IMF. Rather, it is a potential claim on the freely usable currencies of IMF members. SDRs can be exchanged for these currencies. The value of the SDR is based on a basket of five currencies—the U.S. dollar, the euro, the Chinese renminbi, the Japanese yen, and the British pound sterling."

This is a neutral reserve currency, already created and managed by the IMF, and used to a small degree in global reserve transactions between central banks. However, as many point out, the IMF is a clearly westernized organization, controlled mostly by the United States, and thus is not truly neutral-oppositional countries like Russia and China would still dislike an SDR based world, although there are some benefits. Namely, each country would be able to continue to use, issue, and control their own local currency, using SDRs instead for global trade and converting back to their own currency when needed. However, given that SDRs would be cleared through the IMF, there is still the potential for economic warfare in the same manner that was imposed on Russia in the early stages of the Ukraine invasion- a complete freeze and seizure of reserves, rendering the asset virtually useless. It may be easy to get Western countries to agree to this new system, but others will likely be wary. The second option is a return to a semi floating gold standard- each country re-backs their currencies to gold and opts for floating exchange rates between currencies, and in order to ensure smooth functioning, everyone must allow free trade and redemption of gold, even between antagonistic member states.

SANTIAGO CAPITAL
G8 Countries, China & Switzerland Monetary Aggregates vs Gold Reserves

Monetary Aggregates (Local Currency)

	Country	Exchange Rate ($US)	M0 (Local)	M1 (Local)	M2 (Local)
1	Canada	1.2552	$397,019,000,000	$1,583,776,000,000	$2,389,771,000,000
2	China	6.3528	¥9,080,000,000,000	¥64,740,000,000,000	¥238,290,000,000,000
3	France				
4	Germany				
5	Italy				
	Euro	1.1411	€6,109,700,000,000	€11,155,921,000,000	€14,584,944,000,000
6	Japan	114.1900	¥111,928,200,000,000	¥995,226,300,000,000p	¥1,178,592,300,000,000
7	Russia	76.4817	12,954,200,000,000p	34,544,570,000,000p	62,312,500,000,000p
8	Switzerland	0.9140	CHF 736,944,000,000	CHF 767,622,000,000	CHF 1,095,369,000,000
9	UK	1.3675	£95,157,000,000	£2,363,869,000,000	£3,495,651,000,000
10	US	1.0000	$6,394,800,000,000	$20,345,000,000,000	$21,436,700,000,000

Monetary Aggregates ($US Equivalent)

	Country	Gold (Tons)	M0 ($US)	M1 ($US)	M2 ($US)
1	Canada	-	$416,299,394,519	$1,260,975,143,401	$1,824,228,051,172
2	China*	1,948	$1,429,291,021,282	$10,190,782,017,378	$37,509,444,654,326
3	France	2,436			
4	Germany	3,359			
5	Italy	2,452			
	Euro	8,752	$6,971,778,670,000	$12,730,021,453,100	$16,642,879,598,600
6	Japan	846	$997,767,329,889	$8,715,527,629,390	$10,319,575,269,288
7	Russia	2,299	$169,476,465,720	$451,671,053,337	$814,737,381,622
8	Switzerland	1,040	$806,284,463,895	$839,849,015,317	$1,198,434,354,086
9	UK	310	$130,127,197,500	$3,233,590,857,500	$4,780,302,742,500
10	US	8,134	$6,394,800,000,000	$20,345,000,000,000	$21,436,700,000,000
	Total	31,576	$17,215,664,542,304	$57,766,417,169,425	$94,526,302,012,094

Gold price needed to back each country's Monetary Aggregates

	Country	Gold (Ounces)	M0 (Gold $)	M1 (Gold $)	M2 (Gold $)
1	Canada		NA	NA	NA
2	China*	62,640,540	$22,854	$162,947	$599,762
3	France	78,202,780			
4	Germany	107,940,695			
5	Italy	78,721,460			
	G8 Euro Area	280,982,960	$24,812	$45,305	$59,231
6	Japan	27,180,830	$36,733	$320,886	$379,943
7	Russia	73,809,395	$2,295	$6,119	$11,038
8	Switzerland	33,389,200	$24,148	$25,153	$35,893
9	UK	9,962,550	$13,075	$324,800	$480,309
10	US	261,498,000	$24,454	$77,802	$81,972
	Total	1,014,103,410	$16,976	$56,963	$93,212

Source: M0, M1 and M2 via www.tradingeconomics.com. Euro Area M0 via Bloomberg. Dates as of October-December 2021
Gold Reserves via World Gold Council as of October/November 2021
Euro Area Gold reserves figure includes France, Germany, Italy as well as the ECBs Gold holdings of 505 tons
Exchange Rate as of January 15, 2022
Assumes 32,165 ounces of gold / ton and a current gold price of $1,818
* There is widely held belief that China has more gold reserves than currently reported

Brent Johnson of Santiago Capital put together this great table-illustrating the price at which gold would have to be to re-back their monetary supply. To back M2 Money Supply in the US, gold would have to be priced at around $82k an ounce, whereas Russia could achieve the same backing for just $11k an ounce. This is what would be called a floating gold exchange standard- where each country would store gold as reserves and use it for redemptions of their own currency. Russia and China are preparing for a system like this, evidenced by their massive dumpings of U.S. Treasury positions and steady acquisitions of gold for their central bank vaults.

However, although this system worked *somewhat* well in the past, I simply do not believe we will return to it. This is due to multiple factors, but the largest being the inconvenience, difficulty, and trust required to continually move gold between central banks, banks, and individuals, along with the frequent bank runs that will occur on banks that over issue currency without sufficient gold to back it. Gold is money, in many ways- it is difficult to use for small transactions and must be centralized. You can't take an ounce of gold to the store to buy groceries; and shaving small pieces off a nugget to pay for goods isn't something that is likely to happen in our post-modern, digitized world. The same thing that happened last time will happen again.

They will re-back the currency 1:1 with gold. They'll issue paper banknotes as claims against the gold. Once enough time has passed, they will slowly start to increase the supply of banknotes. 1.5:1, then 2:1, then 3:1. Once everyone finally realizes again that the currency has been inflated, and their value has been stolen, they can re-value the price of a gold to a new higher price and restart the process all over again. The fundamental issue is trust- we have to give over large portions of gold to centralized entities for convenience and payment facilitation, but we have to trust that they will not print more paper currency than what can be backed.

This leads me to the third major option for what I believe can be a new world reserve currency- Bitcoin.

Bitcoin is a peer to peer, decentralized cryptocurrency that can send and receive value without a single trusted third party. Instead, Bitcoin relies on a network of nodes and miners to confirm and validate transactions, and then to record them in a block, which is appended to the most recent block- thus creating a "blockchain". Since its inception in 2009, Bitcoin has established itself as the most durable, long-lasting, and resilient cryptocurrency to date. Bitcoin mining is a process that involves a distributed consensus system, which is used to confirm pending transactions by adding them to the blockchain. This process ensures that transactions are processed in a chronological order and protects the neutrality of the network. It also allows computers on the network to agree on the current state of the system. In order for a transaction to be confirmed, it must be included in a block that follows strict cryptographic rules that are verified by the network. These rules prevent previous blocks from being altered, as this would invalidate all subsequent blocks.

Total computational power of the network has steadily increased since inception, making the network more and more secure over time- and although Bitcoin is slow to adapt and change, and perhaps even behind in smart contract development, many extoll this as a virtue. Any monetary network that has the properties of hard money, such as gold, must also be resistant to change, even "good" change as almost all changes are tradeoffs and create winners and losers. If Bitcoin did eventually become the new world reserve currency, it's value would be incalculable. There can only ever be 21 million Bitcoins- and divide the entire global GDP, asset base, and consumer goods by this figure and you see astronomical figures for a single Bitcoin. Imagine reducing the entire global money supply to $21M- a house could cost $0.50, a car 2c, a sandwich thousandths of a penny.

This is not a Bitcoin paper- there are authors much more intelligent than I with writings already in this area, such as Saifedean Ammous' "Bitcoin Standard". However, I would recommend looking further into it. For all the Ethereum maxis out here, I also am not saying that Ether is worthless, or has no intrinsic value. From a pure monetary economics standpoint, Bitcoin is a harder money- harder to change and more difficult to update; and thus is much more likely to be used as a global reserve currency than Ethereum is. It is just to say that for most countries, inexperienced in crypto and wary of control of monetary systems by powerful interests like the United States, are unlikely to choose systems wrapped with complexity and hard-to-grasp concepts. They are more likely to choose cryptocurrencies with robust security, (relatively) simple protocols, hard supply caps, and a proven network effect- and Bitcoin has all of these. Bitcoin's second layer, the Lightning Network, which will be used to facilitate the daily payments that make up 99% of the transactions in the financial system, is steadily growing. Lightning wallets are getting easier, cheaper, and more convenient to use by the day. Although there is not enough throughput on the base chain to support a global payment network, there is potentially on Lightning. Base chain transactions can be used for large purchases, like bank transfers or movement of funds for a land purchase, while the second layer can be used for shopping, ecommerce, microloans, etc. Several countries have already adopted Bitcoin as legal tender and are implementing Lightning wallets as payment options for small businesses.

(The above statements are my opinion, and are thus subject to change. I am far from an expert on cryptocurrencies, Bitcoin or otherwise. I recommend doing your own research before you invest any funds into any token)

Hyperinflation can't happen here. It's never occurred in a developed country, especially one like the US.

This is another common retort. Almost everyone in the West suffers from recency bias; our monetary system has been stable the last 50 years- why can't it be stable for the next 50, or 100? Stability has only been achieved through the creation of a system that has built in demand for dollars- and anytime systemic risk has popped up through a crisis, we have kicked the can up the stairs by papering over the crisis with more debt. At a certain point the debt becomes far too unsustainable and the entire system either melts down or up.

Secondly, you're wrong- this has occurred before in American history. The Richmond Fed posted a research paper explaining the basic process by which the Confederacy, the Southern antagonists during the Civil War, began turning to the printing press to finance the heavy costs of war against the North.[86] The South was mostly agrarian, and lacked the industrial and financial centers of their counterpart. Thus, they were unable to borrow the massive sums needed to finance their war effort, and worse still, they lacked the centralized power to crack down on member states to cough up enough resources to fully pay for the war.

The early stages of the war saw rampant inflation as the Confederate government readily printed more to fund the rapidly rising war costs. However, it was not until the later stages of the war, where significant Union victories and destruction of Confederate infrastructure really began to damage public confidence in the currency. Although the money supply had grown by 2000x, prices climbed above 9,000x their 1861 levels as monetary velocity exploded and suspicions regarding the South's defeat grew to be widespread. In such a world, Southerners knew their newfangled money would become worthless. Our founding fathers warned against banks and centralized control of money supply. Andrew Jackson went so far as to claim that bankers were those who "gambled on the breadstuffs of the country, and when they won, took the profits, but when they lost, charged it to the bank". He spitefully called

them "a den of vipers and thieves".
Jefferson went even further:[87]

"If the American people ever allow private banks to control the
issue of their currency, first by inflation, then by deflation, the
banks and corporations that will grow up around [the banks]
will deprive the people of all property until their children wake-
up homeless on the continent their fathers conquered."

There were only two ways he believed that a nation could
be enslaved- by sword or by debt. When these debts finally
come due, the unfortunate government response is to print
any cash necessary to stave off default. It was stealing from
the future, from the prosperity of our children- the most
immoral of ventures. Thomas Jefferson was concerned that
the creation of a national bank would lead to the formation
of a financial monopoly that could harm state banks. He also
believed that such a bank might adopt policies that favored
creditors, such as financiers and merchants, over debtors, such
as plantation owners and family farmers. Jefferson believed
that this could create inequities and undermine the interests of
certain groups within society. In addition to his concerns about
the potential impact of a national bank on state banks and
the interests of different groups within society, he also argued
that the Constitution did not give the government the power

to create corporations, including a national bank. Despite these objections, the bill proposed by Alexander Hamilton to establish a national bank eventually passed through both the House and the Senate after a prolonged debate.

President Washington signed the bill into law in February 1791. The National Bank served as the financial agent for the federal government, performing a number of important functions including collecting tax revenues, safeguarding government funds, lending money to the government, transferring government deposits through its network of branches, and paying the government's bills. The bank also managed the payment of interest on U.S. government securities held by European investors. Overall, the National Bank played a crucial role in the financial operations of the U.S. government.

The U.S. government, which held the largest share in the National Bank, did not directly manage the bank but did receive a portion of its profits. The Treasury Secretary was given the power to review the bank's financial records, request regular updates on its financial condition, and move the government's deposits out of the bank at any time for any reason. To prevent inflation and maintain transparency, the National Bank was not allowed to purchase U.S. government bonds.[88] These measures were put in place to ensure that the bank operated in a responsible and accountable manner.

The Federal Reserve's current program is one almost exclusively of purchasing Treasury bonds- and manipulating market interest rates through the fixing of the funds rate, "Dot Plot" estimations, and forward guidance. The current iteration is a perversion of even what a central bank in Jefferson's time was created to do. Any illusion of separation of money and state is gone, and the Fed, owned by private corporations, exists solely to uphold the banking system and the governmental apparatus that protects it. Over two hundred years ago, Jefferson issued a dire warning. The truth was obfuscated with decades of faulty economic theory and QE pumping financial assets. We never listened. Now we must deal with the tyrannical, rent-seeking banking apparatus that has an iron grip over politics, economics and trade.

The Revolution will not be televised.

BIBLIOGRAPHY

[1] Cole, Chris. "Volatility and the Allegory of the Prisoner's Dilemma." *https://www.artemiscm.com/*, 11 Mar. 2019, artemiscm.docsend.com/view/t2rpfyivddgqg6n8.

[2] Wen, Yi, and Brian Reinbold. "The Changing Relationship Between Trade and America's Gold Reserves." *St. Louis Fed*, 9 Dec. 2021, www.stlouisfed.org/publications/regional-economist/first-quarter-2020/changing-relationship-trade-americas-gold-reserves.

[3] McKinnon, Ronald. "A NEW TRIPARTITE MONETARY AGREEMENT OR a LIMPING DOLLAR STANDARD." *https://ies.princeton.edu/*, Oct. 1974, ies.princeton.edu/pdf/E106.pdf.

[4] Ghizoni, By Sandra Kollen. "Nixon Ends Convertibility of U.S. Dollars to Gold and Announces Wage/Price Controls."

Federal Reserve History, www.federalreservehistory.org/ essays/gold-convertibility-ends.

[5] "U.S. Dollar Index - 43 Year Historical Chart." *MacroTrends*, www.macrotrends.net/1329/us-dollar-index-historical-chart.

[6] "Birth of Petrodollar." *Great Power Relations*, 8 Dec. 2020, greatpowerrelations.com/great-powers/status-of-great-powers/key-drivers-of-economic-capabilities/dollar-and-de-dollarization/birth-of-petrodollar.

[7] "Inflation, Consumer Prices for the United States." *Fred Economic Data*, 3 May 2022, fred.stlouisfed.org/series/ FPCPITOTLZGUSA.

[8] *International Affairs: The U.S.-Saudi Arabian Joint Commission on Economic Cooperation - Government Accountability Office (GAO) Report*. www.legistorm.com/reports/view/ gao/6895/ The_U_S_Saudi_Arabian_Joint_Commission_on_Economi c_Cooperation.html.

[9] Nomisma digital. "List of Central Banks of the World." *Faisal*

Khan, 5 Oct. 2022, faisalkhan.com/solutions/banking/list-of-central-banks-of-the-world.

[10] Bernanke, Ben. "The Dollar's International Role: An 'Exorbitant Privilege'?" Brookings, 29 July 2016, www.brookings.edu/blog/ben-bernanke/2016/01/07/the-dollars-international-role-an-exorbitant-privilege-2.

[11] Smith, Sidd. "How Does the United States Export Inflation?" *What Is Money*, 7 Oct. 2022, whatismoney.info/exporting-inflation.

[12] Reinbold, Brian, and Yi Wen. "Understanding the Roots of the U.S. Trade Deficit." *St. Louis Fed*, 9 Dec. 2021, www.stlouisfed.org/publications/regional-economist/third-quarter-2018/understanding-roots-trade-deficit.

[13] Siripurapu, Anshu. "The Dollar: The World's Currency." *Council on Foreign Relations*, 29 Sept. 2020, www.cfr.org/backgrounder/dollar-worlds-currency.

[14] Lim, Jie-Hui, and Delphine Masquelier. "Worldwide Currency

Usage and Trends." *Swift.com*, Dec. 2015, www.swift.com/ node/19186#:~:text=The%20US%20dollar %20dominates%20as,regional%20currency%20usage %20in%20value.

[15] Daya, Mehul, and Neels Heyneke. "THE RISE AND FALL OF THE EURODOLLAR SYSTEM." *www.nedbank.co.za*, Sept. 2016, www.nedbank.co.za/content/dam/nedbank-crp/ reports/Strategy/NeelsAndMehul/2016/September/ TheRiseAndFallOfTheEurodollarSystem_160907.pdf.

[16] Cole, Chris. "Volatility and the Alchemy of Risk." *Artemis Capital*, Oct. 2017, artemiscm.docsend.com/ view/2b34894bzsaqsbcx.

[17] Holton, Glynn. "History of Value-at-Risk: 1922-1998." *Wharton Business School*, July 2002, stat.wharton.upenn.edu/~steele/ Courses/434/434Context/RiskManagement/ VaRHistlory.pdf.

[18] Peruvian Bull. "Dow Jones Industrial Average." *TradingView*, July 2021, www.tradingview.com/chart/X3N7yOqJ/?

symbol=TVC:DJI.

[19] Patterson, Scott. *Quants: The Maths Geniuses Who Brought Down Wall Street*. Random House Business Books, 2023.

[20] Eckblad, By Donald Bernhardt And Marshall. "Stock Market Crash of 1987." *Federal Reserve History*, www.federalreservehistory.org/essays/stock-market-crash-of-1987.

[21] Patterson, Scott. *Quants: The Maths Geniuses Who Brought Down Wall Street*. Random House Business Books, 2023.

[22] Trimbath, Susanne. *Naked, Short and Greedy: Wall Street's Failure to Deliver*. Spiramus Press, 2019.

[23] Merrick, John J, et al. "Strategic Trading Behavior and Price Distortion in a Manipulated Market: Anatomy of a Squeeze." *City University of New York*, Jan. 2003, static1.squarespace.com/static/555266c0e4b008b6a4552c3a/t/55626e5ae4b004a8dfc8288d/1432514138731/Gilt_Squeeze_final.pdf.

[24] *OTC Derivatives Statistics at end-June 2019*. 8 Nov. 2019,

www.bis.org/publ/otc_hy1911.htm.

[25] Bird, Mike. "Understanding Deutsche Bank's $47

Trillion Derivatives Book." *WSJ*, 5 Oct. 2016,

www.wsj.com/articles/does-deutsche-bank-have-

a-47-trillion-derivatives-problem-1475689629.

[26] Council on Foreign Relations. "Panic: The Untold Story

of the 2008 Financial Crisis | Full VICE Special Report

| HBO." *YouTube*, 1 May 2019, www.youtube.com/

watch?v=QozGSS7QY_U.

[27] ---. "Volatility of an Impossible Object." *Artemis Capital*,

Sept.   2012,   artemiscm.docsend.com/

view/74nw2t766wnvnuwj.

[28] "Fractional Reserve Banking." *Mercatus Center*,

28 June 2012, www.mercatus.org/research/federal-

testimonies/fractional-reserve-banking.

[29] Choudhary, Manish. "Economy and Short Term Debt Cycles (Part-2)." *Get Money Rich*, Apr. 2019, getmoneyrich.com/economy-and-short-term-debt-cycles.

[30]   Richardson,   By   Gary.   "Banking Panics   of   1930-31."   *Federal   Reserve History*,   www.federalreservehistory.org/essays/banking-panics-1930-31.

[31] "Federal Debt: Total Public Debt as Percent of Gross Domestic Product." *FRED Economic Data*, 22 Dec. 2022, fred.stlouisfed.org/series/GFDEGDQ188S.

[32] "Assets: Total Assets: Total Assets (Less Eliminations From Consolidation): Wednesday Level." *FRED Economic Data*, 5 Jan. 2023, fred.stlouisfed.org/series/WALCL.

[33] Schwartzer, Lyn Alden. "Money-Printing: 2020 Vs. 2008." *SeekingAlpha*, 6 Nov. 2020, seekingalpha.com/

article/4384862-money-printing-2020-vs-2008.

[34] Anderson, Richard, and Charles Gascon. *A Closer Look: Assistance Programs in the Wake of the Crisis.* 9 Dec. 2021, www.stlouisfed.org/publications/regional-economist/january-2011/a-closer-look-brassistance-programs-in-the-wake-of-the-crisis.

[35] Pisani, Bob. "Wealth Gap Grows as Rising Corporate Profits Boost Stock Holdings Controlled by Richest Households." *CNBC,* 27 Aug. 2020, www.cnbc.com/2020/08/27/wealth-gap-grows-as-rising-corporate-profits-boost-stock-holdings-controlled-by-richest-households.html.

[36] "Shares of Gross Domestic Product: Personal Consumption Expenditures." *FRED Economic Data,* 27 Oct. 2022, fred.stlouisfed.org/series/DPCERE1Q156NBEA.

[37] Hanson, Melanie. "Student Loan Debt Statistics."

Education   Data   Initiative, 1   Jan.   2023,

educationdata.org/student-loan-debt-statistics.

[38]   Lynch,   David.   "Fears   of   Corporate   Debt

Bomb   Grow   as   Coronavirus   Outbreak

Worsens." *Washington   Post*, 10   Mar.   2020,

www.washingtonpost.com/business/2020/03/10/

coronavirus-markets-economy-corporate-debt.

[39]   "The   State   of   the   American   Debt-Slaves   Q2

2020:   The   Credit   Card   Phenomenon." *Wolf

Street*, 9   Aug.   2020,   wolfstreet.com/2020/08/09/

the-state-of-the-american-debt-slaves-q2-2020-the-

credit-card-phenomenon.

[40] "Motor   Vehicle   Loans   Owned   and   Securitized." *FRED

Economic   Data*, 9   Jan.   2023,   fred.stlouisfed.org/

series/MVLOAS.

[41]   Prabhu,   Siddharth.   "LONG-TERM   CAPITAL

MANAGEMENT: THE DANGERS OF LEVERAGE." *Duke*

University, sites.duke.edu/djepapers/files/2016/08/prabhu.pdf.

[42] Harbert, Tam. "Here's How Much the 2008 Bailouts Really Cost." *MIT Sloan*, 21 Feb. 2019, mitsloan.mit.edu/ideas-made-to-matter/heres-how-much-2008-bailouts-really-cost.

[43] Rabouin, Dion. "Global Debt Soars to 356% of GDP." *Axios*, 18 Feb. 2021, www.axios.com/2021/02/18/global-debt-gdp.

[44] "The 2020 Long-Term Budget Outlook." *Congressional Budget Office*, 21 Sept. 2020, www.cbo.gov/publication/56598.

[45] "Deficit Tracker." *Bipartisan Policy Center*, bipartisanpolicy.org/report/deficit-tracker.

[46] "Federal Funds Effective Rate." *FRED Economic Data*, 3 Jan. 2023, fred.stlouisfed.org/series/FEDFUNDS.

[47] Cheung, Brian. "Here's What Powell Said That Seems to

Be Troubling Markets." *Yahoo Finance*, Dec. 2018, www.yahoo.com/now/powell-said-seems-troubling-markets-181403220.html.

[48] Domm, Patti. "Fed Chief Powell Gave the Markets the Message They Wanted." *CNBC*, 4 Jan. 2019, www.cnbc.com/2019/01/04/fed-chief-powell-just-walked-back-his-autopilot-remark-and-the-financial-markets-love-it.html.

[49] VON WACHTER, TILL M., and ARNE L. KALLEBERG. "The U.S. Labor Market During and After the Great Recession: Continuities and Transformations." *National Library of Medicine*, May 2018, www.ncbi.nlm.nih.gov/pmc/articles/PMC5959048.

[50] ---. "Volatility at World's End." *Artemis Capital*, Mar. 2012, artemiscm.docsend.com/view/u8q6ygn3h8j5w99f.

[51] Wang, Joseph. *Central Banking 101.* Joseph, 2021.

[52] Staff, Reuters. "Iran to Accept Payment in Gold From Trading Partners." *U.S.*, 29 Feb. 2012, www.reuters.com/article/us-iran-oil-payment/iran-to-accept-payment-in-gold-from-trading-partners-idUSTRE81S0GU20120229.

[53] Gromen, Luke, and Tyler Tichelaar. *The Mr. X Interviews Volume 2: World Views From a Fictional US Sovereign Creditor.* Aviva Publishing, 2020.

[54] Hebner, Kevin. "The Dollar Is Our Currency, but It's Your Problem." *IPE*, 11 Mar. 2020, www.ipe.com/the-dollar-is-our-currency-but-its-your-problem/25599.article.

[55] Alden, Lyn. "The Fraying of the US Global Currency Reserve System." *Lyn Alden*, 8 July 2022, www.lynalden.com/fraying-petrodollar-system.

[56] "Federal Debt Held by Foreign and International Investors." *FRED Economic Data*, 3 Dec. 2022,

fred.stlouisfed.org/series/FDHBFIN.

[57] "U.S. Net International Investment Position." *FRED Economic Data*, 29 Dec. 2022, fred.stlouisfed.org/series/IIPUSNETIQ.

[58] Gromen, Luke, and Tyler Tichelaar. *The Mr. X Interviews Volume 2: World Views From a Fictional US Sovereign Creditor*. Aviva Publishing, 2020.

[59] Gromen, Luke, and Tyler Tichelaar. *The Mr. X Interviews Volume 2: World Views From a Fictional US Sovereign Creditor*. Aviva Publishing, 2020.

[60] Gromen, Luke. "FFTT Tree Rings - a Compilation of Critical Data Points." *FFTT Tree Rings*, 7 Oct. 2022, fftt-treerings.com.

[61] Baklanova, Viktoria, et al. "Primer: Money Market Funds and the Repo Market." *SEC.gov*, Feb. 2021, www.sec.gov/files/mmfs-and-the-repo-market-021721.pdf.

[62] ---. "The Fraying of the US Global Currency Reserve System." *Lyn Alden*, 8 July 2022, www.lynalden.com/ fraying-petrodollar-system.

[63] Bordo, Michael, and Robert McCauley. "Triffin: Dilemma or Myth?" *Bank for International Settlements*, Dec. 2017, www.bis.org/publ/work684.pdf.

[64] Real Vision Finance. "The 'Dollar Milkshake' Theory With Brent Johnson." *YouTube*, 9 Feb. 2019, www.youtube.com/watch?v=vDr3lRZ01Zo.

[65] ---. "Volatility at World's End." *Artemis Capital*, Mar. 2012, artemiscm.docsend.com/view/ u8q6ygn3h8j5w99f.

[66] *DollarDaze Economic Commentary Blog - Gold, Oil, Stocks, Investments, Currencies, and the Federal Reserve.* web.archive.org/web/20090116163658/ http:/dollardaze.org/blog/?page_id=00017.

[67] "Loans and Leases in Bank Credit, All Commercial Banks." *FRED Economic Data*, 13 Jan. 2023, fred.stlouisfed.org/series/TOTLL.

[68] Pettinger, Tejvan. "Debt Spiral Explained." *Economics Help*, 22 Jan. 2020, www.economicshelp.org/blog/5118/economics/debt-spiral-explained.

[69] Edwards, Chris. "Federal Debt and Unfunded Entitlement Promises." *CATO Institute*, www.cato.org/blog/federal-debt-unfunded-entitlement-promises.

[70] Rugy, Veronique de. "A Comprehensive Look at US Debt." *Mercatus Center*, Sept. 2013, www.mercatus.org/media/54876/download.

[71] "Federal Budgeting." *U.S. GAO*, 23 Mar. 2021, www.gao.gov/federal-budgeting.

[72] "Budget of the U.S. Government." *WhiteHouse.gov*, Dec.

2021,   www.whitehouse.gov/wp-content/
uploads/2021/05/budget_fy22.pdf.

[73] Townsend, Erik, and Luke Gromen. "Luke Gromen: The
U.S. Government Cannot Afford Secular Inflation."
Macrovoices.com,   www.macrovoices.com/guest-
content/list-guest-transcripts/4399-2021-10-21-
transcript-of-the-podcast-interview-between-erik-
townsend-and-luke-gromen/file.

[74] Brettell, Karen, and Davide Barbuscia. "U.S. Treasury
Asks Major Banks if It Should Buy Back Bonds." *Yahoo
Finance*, Oct. 2022, www.yahoo.com/video/us-
treasury-asks-major-banks-162152288.html.

[75] ---. "Panic: The Untold Story of the 2008 Financial Crisis
| Full VICE Special Report | HBO." *YouTube*, 1 May
2019, www.youtube.com/watch?v=QozGSS7QY_U.

[76] Fujikawa, Megumi. "Japan Bond Market Sets Record for
No Trades." *WSJ*, 12 Oct. 2022, www.wsj.com/

articles/japan-bond-market-sets-record-for-nothing-happening-11665576046.

[77] *The Behavior of Money Velocity in High and Low Inflation Countries on JSTOR.* www.jstor.org/stable/3839075.

[78] Kevin Muir. "Neel Kashkari Unlimited Fed Printing." *YouTube- 60 Minutes,* 23 Mar. 2020, www.youtube.com/watch?v=DUrlNHTxuJM.

[79] Pettis, Michael. "How Does Excessive Debt Hurt an Economy?" *Carnegie Endowment for International Peace,* carnegieendowment.org/chinafinancialmarkets/86397.

[80] ---. "Two Tiered Monetary System." *Fed Guy,* 25 Jan. 2021, fedguy.com/two-tiered-monetary-system.

[81] *Consumer Prices up 7.5 Percent Over Year Ended January 2022: The Economics Daily: U.S. Bureau of Labor Statistics.* 16 Feb. 2022, www.bls.gov/opub/ted/2022/consumer-prices-up-7-5-percent-over-

year-ended-january-2022.htm.

[82] "Velocity of M2 Money Stock." *FRED Economic Data*, 22 Dec. 2022, fred.stlouisfed.org/series/M2V.

[83] "---." *U.S. GAO*, 23 Mar. 2021, www.gao.gov/federal-budgeting.

[84] "American Billionaires by the Numbers." *Americans for Tax Fairness*, americansfortaxfairness.org/billionaires.

[85] *International Monetary Fund.* 1 Aug. 2016, www.imf.org/external/error.htm?URL=https://www.imf.org/en/About/Factsheets/Sheets/2016/08/01/14/51/Special-Drawing-Right-SDR.

[86] "Monetary Policy in the Confederacy." *Richmond Federal Reserve*, Oct. 2005, www.richmondfed.org/-/media/richmondfedorg/publications/research/econ_focus/2005/fall/pdf/economic_history.pdf.

[87] Beisner, Tom. "Thomas Jefferson's Top 10 Quotes on Money and Banking." *The Whitlock Co.*, 18 Aug. 2021, www.whitlockco.com/thomas-jeffersons-top-10-quotes-on-money-and-banking.

[88] Hill, By Andrew. "The First Bank of the United States." *Federal Reserve History*, www.federalreservehistory.org/essays/first-bank-of-the-us.

ACKNOWLEDGEMENT

I dedicate this work to my family, dear friends, and those who have supported me throughout this journey. When I first published Part 1 of Dollar Endgame in the summer of 2021, I truly did not know what to expect. The outpouring of interest, support, and intellectual debate was humbling for me, and I did my best to answer and think as critically as possible. I would not be here today if it weren't for my family- especially my dad, who allowed me to bounce ideas off him for hours and come back with his typical scientific critiques and rebuttals. I have been plagued with the ideas in this book for years now, and to get them out on paper has been cathartic.

The injustice, cruelty and tyranny of the system was never lost on me. In my cold dorm room in the Pacific Northwest, I began a one man crusade 6 years ago to uncover the truth about our financial system and to try to imagine one that would bring life, hope, and prosperity to the People. This journey led to me reading hundreds of books, analyzing research papers, debating economics and finance professors, and listening to thousands of hours of podcasts and videos. I traveled across the world, meeting with equity traders and Managing Directors in New York; entrepreneurs and business owners in Washington; and federal government officials in California.

2008 was a watershed moment that opened my eyes to the corruption and rot within our financial system. It infuriated me in a way that is hard to describe. I was born with an extremely strong sense of justice, and the perversion that took place in back room deals in October and November of 2008 was something that violated me to my core. I imagined myself as a Knight on a crusade against an evil that few could see, and even fewer could understand. My obsession with understanding the system could only be compared to religious fervor.

In 2018 I met the former Chairman and CEO of Countrywide Financial Angelo Mozilo, the man at the helm of one of the largest mortgage originators in the United States, only to hear him begin a several hours long rant about how he and his team were not responsible for the Subprime Mortgage Crisis. I do not know what I thought going into that meeting- but I assumed that he would be repentant, sorrowful somehow. I thought he would acknowledge his role- perhaps he did know the scope of the treachery that Wall Street was playing; the scale of the derivatives monster it was creating on the backs of the mortgages he created.

I still believed he would see what he did was wrong; that he was not a scapegoat in this scandal, but also a participant. One who benefited financially from the disaster. I was sadly mistaken. My discussions with those in government were no different. It seemed that most of them were caught completely unawares by the calamity, and just flew by the seat of their pants and took their indications from those in the banking industry. When I asked Rosie Rios, Treasurer of the United States in 2019 what being in the midst of the Financial crisis was like, she responded by stating it was pure chaos. No one, even at the Federal level, knew what they were doing.

Somehow, I think this was a kernel of truth among the deluge of lies; most in government, media and even academia are uneducated about the true nature of economics and finance. They are either fooled by those truly in power, or they obfuscate the truth for themselves as they do not want to know. It's hard to get someone to understand something when their very job depends on not understanding it. The lies, sophisms, and fallacies have infiltrated every corner of our governmental and educational institutions. This only benefits the power-hungry financial elites who really understand how our economic machine operates, and how to game it for themselves.

The robbery that has occurred, and will continue to occur, was monumental in scale. No one, even I, understood the treachery that was being done by those in high places. Aesop once said, **"We hang the petty thieves and appoint the great ones to public office."** Nothing has changed since 2008- in fact, the corruption, bribery and grift has only become worse. Those who run the system have grown more brazen in their crimes. The fundamental problem is trusting humans, fallible creatures, to govern and control aspects of our life, especially our financial life.

True knowledge is a journey; very few will even attempt it. Curiosity is the first kindling needed to begin a flame of understanding. The truth is the antidote to chaos, and is vital in beginning the process of resetting our economic life to one approximating freedom, individual liberty, and human value. My prayer is that this book somehow moves the needle in this direction.

Thank you all, and Power to the Players.

~Peruvian Bull

Made in the USA
Monee, IL
20 February 2023

28356302R00142